SAS EVANGELIST

AN EPIC STORY OF ONE MAN'S JOURNEY OF DEATH TO LIFE

KEVIN CHARLES-THOMPSON

WWW.SASEVANGELIST.COM

CONTENTS

1. Into The Storm — 9
2. Standby Standby — 14
3. Find Him — 20
4. A Special Breed Of Men — 30
5. Selection — 38
6. Born A Rebel — 48
7. Across The Water — 56
8. Fallen World — 64
9. Pirates — 74
10. The Wild West — 80
11. Three Years — 86
12. The New Front Line — 96
13. Strongholds — 108
14. Seven Devils Part 1 — 114
15. The Seven Devils — 118
16. Seven Devils Part 2 — 122
17. What Is Truth Part 1 — 128
18. The Word Became Flesh — 136
19. You Must Be Born Again — 138
20. For God So Loved The World — 142
21. The Authority Of The Son — 144
22. I Am The Light Of The World — 146
23. What Is Truth Part 2 — 148
24. Up The Mountain — 156
25. The Cross — 161
26. About The Author — 166
27. About The Book — 172
28. Dedication — 176

PEN Y FAN, BRECON BEACONS

At the final point of the 886-meter climb stands Jacob's ladder that leads to the top of the mountain, an epic physical and mental test of every SAS man during the infamous 'Fan Dance' on SAS selection.

"Jacobs ladder the connection between heaven and earth."

CHAPTER ONE
INTO THE STORM

"Ten Minutes, Ten Minutes!" was shouted down the helicopter as I got tapped on my leg by a teammate sitting next to me. It was time! The door gunner had now lowered the helicopter tailgate as he moved to get into position on the rear-facing heavy machine gun. There was now an icy cold breeze coming down the inside of the helicopter.

My dog Sep, a Belgian Malinois, also known as Septicus Maximus, sat up next to me and started to nudge my leg with his nose. He'd been flat out asleep for the last hour and a half of the flight laying across my boots, trying to keep himself warm. I turned on my wrist GPS, drank some water from my camelback, and slipped a few dog biscuits into his mouth.

I stood up and stretched off after sitting on a cargo net seat with my body armour and helmet on for the last few hours. "Time to go again, into the storm," I thought to myself as I started to take my warm insulated padded jacket off and, using a large black carabiner, I attached it to the cargo net where I had been sitting ready for the flight back. Going out every night non-stop, I had lost track of how many times we had been on the ground during this deployment. Again, we were heading deep into the badlands of Helmand province, Afghanistan.

I had been deployed to Afghanistan before, and I had lost many friends fighting the Taliban. It had been a long campaign that had begun in the wake of 9/11 in 2001. Afghanistan, plagued by war for over thirty years since the Soviet invasion in 1979. Afghanistan was tough; it was an extremely hostile nation, and for us, it was simple, high-risk offensive operations fighting the Taliban.

We arrived during an epic winter; it was freezing, unlike anything I had experienced before. At nighttime, the temperature would drop to around 0c; in the mountains, the temperature could drop below -25c. As we came through the winter, one thing that certainly hit me hard was the extreme Afghan summer. The temperature shift from winter was immense; some days, the temperatures would rise to around 50c, which proved to be brutal for daylight patrols, especially when we encountered the Taliban.

Getting into a gun battle with the Taliban was no easy feat; they would stand their ground and fight. The thing to note here is that the Taliban were war-torn seasoned fighters fighting for a cause that they believed very strongly. They knew the ground well on which they fought and often had locals supporting them. As we approached an area of Taliban fighters, they would get warned that we were coming from the locals keeping watch, which we called 'dickers.' Resulting in an ambush-style attack on our patrols.

> ...the Taliban were war-torn seasoned fighters fighting for a cause that they believed very strongly!

Some of the ferocious gun battles we were involved in often lasted for hours during the scorching heat as we tried to gain a tactical advantage. We would often get attacked by a barrage of rocket-propelled grenades and the infamous PKM Russian machine gun that could suppress our position. The Taliban had effective long-range snipers pinning us down and preventing us from moving, killing many operators.

They would stand and fight for as long as possible; they would only ever retreat if overwhelmed by air fire-power. We would have to call in combat air support forcing the Taliban to retreat. Often they would leave improvised explosive devices IED's behind for us to stand on or remotely detonate them as they fled. Worst-case scenario, the more extremist fighters would wait for us to get to them, detonating themselves as suicide bombers as we approached their positions, trying to take some of us out.

They would mix with the local population using sympathisers to help them, providing both a place for them to stay with food and medical care if they became injured from the fighting. Even after our patrols had finished, we would frequently get attacked by enemy mortar fire when we would be back in our fortified patrol base. Many of them landed and exploded around the area where we would wash, eat and sleep.

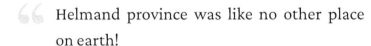 Helmand province was like no other place on earth!

This long history had forged the Taliban into a hard regime of fighters who would stand and fight no matter the cost. It was guerrilla warfare at the highest level. Helmand province was like no other place on earth.

CHAPTER TWO
STANDBY
STANDBY

Tonight's mission was to carry out a detention operation on a senior Taliban commander. He was a high-value target with influence on other senior commanders within the country. He was directly responsible for recruiting, planning, and executing multiple suicide attacks against coalition security forces throughout the Helmand region.

His detention would not only disrupt what the Taliban was planning but would generate new intelligence for us to carry out further detention operations to prevent future enemy attacks. Ultimately, this would destroy the terrorist network within the Helmand region, saving countless innocent lives.

So this was the life of a special force's operator during a long six-month deployment, living the nocturnal life. I lowered my night vision goggles from my helmet and peered through one of the small circular windows of the helicopter out into the night sky, and everything was just green as I stood staring through the goggles. It seemed as if, apart from when I was asleep, I spent more time seeing green than I did daylight.

We flew fast and very low over the desert ground, weaving through the dry arid wadi system that had cut its way through the vast desert mountains.

As I stood facing the tailgate, one of my hands held onto a thin guide wire running above my head down the centre of the helicopter to the tailgate, and my other hand now firmly grasped onto Sep's harness as he was now getting agitated.

"Two Minutes, Two Minutes," was shouted down the line of SAS operators who were now all standing behind one another, ready to go. The sound of the helicopter changed as it banked over to the left and then the right a few times before aggressively reducing speed as I gripped the guide wire tightly, pulling Sep towards me.

Within moments the rear wheels touched the ground, and the squadron launched out, running straight off the tailgate into total darkness. As I leapt off the tailgate with Sep at my side, not phased, he pushed straight past me into the thick dust cloud created by the helicopter's rotors being so close to the ground. We sprinted across the field towards the target. The lead attached directly to Sep's harness from my waist was now completely taut as he dragged me forward, following the rest of the team.

My hands were now on my weapon, staring down my night vision goggles. I could see the other assault teams pushing past us, heading to the different sides of the compound to get into their assault positions—some position themselves on ladders along the compound wall to provide security.

I could hear over the radio the voices of the drone pilots who were providing overwatch; they were giving a readout of any movement seen from within the target compound and the surrounding area as we approached.

 All calls, "Standby, Standby!

As I followed my team across the field, I could now see our approach route to the entrance. It was a wooden door on an outside compound wall, which would take us directly into the main building. As I moved down the compound wall towards the door, I stepped past my teammates, who were now stacked up one behind the other at the doorway, covering the threat. I knelt in front of them while Sep stood, staring right at the door. I raised the camera on the back of his harness and turned on the small monitor attached to the front of my body armour.

Then unclipping the black carabiner of the lanyard that was attaching me to his harness, he was ready to go; this land shark was now focused on one thing, going through that doorway, and dealing with whatever stood on the other side of it.

I could now hear bursts of AK47 machine guns!

All calls, "Standby, Standby!" came over the earpiece of my radio. A few moments later, "Go! Go! Go!" BOOM! Several explosions from various locations went off simultaneously as multiple assault teams moved into the compound. The explosive charge that we had placed over our wooden door had completely disintegrated it into pieces, and it was lying in bits on the ground. Sep, without hesitation, immediately ran inside the building.

I could now hear bursts of AK47 machine guns coming from somewhere else inside the compound and some men shouting in Arabic. Over the radio, I heard that one of our assault teams had come under enemy gunfire as they entered the compound's courtyard from three or four Taliban fighters standing on a neighbouring rooftop.

CHAPTER THREE
FIND HIM

I had followed Sep into the room: it was dark and empty. My other teammates, who followed me, cleared the room. We identified a long passageway with a blanket draped over the entrance, and Sep had already moved down it, clearly following a scent trail. I glanced down at my monitor, and I could see that he was working hard, clearing multiple rooms along the passage, searching for any enemy fighters that may have been hiding.

The fighting continued outside, with more automatic gunfire, and now a few rockets sounding like RPGs (rocket-propelled grenades) had been fired, exploding in the distance. It was clear that a small number of Taliban fighters in a neighbouring compound had come out after hearing the explosions. We followed Sep down the corridor, going from room to room until eventually, we got to a room where the door was closed, and Sep was standing there waiting for us.

> ...Find Him!

The team stacked up behind me as I got ready to send Sep into the room. I gave the nod to my teammate; the door was opened while throwing a flash-bang inside. Bang! Bang! Bang! It went off! As I shouted, "Find Him!" Sep launched into the room, and I immediately followed him in. As I entered the room, I could see that he had jumped straight onto a Taliban fighter who had been holding an AK47 machine gun. He had been standing in the centre of the room, facing the door.

He was getting ready to fire at us as we entered the room, which would have killed me with a long burst from an AK47 machine gun at that short range. He had dropped his weapon on the floor when Sep hit him, knocking him straight to the ground. Sep now firmly held his arm in his mouth and was standing right on top of him, wrestling with him, completely pinning him to the floor. The team had followed me in, clearing the remainder of the room.

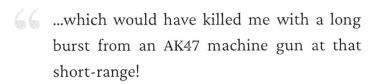

> ...which would have killed me with a long burst from an AK47 machine gun at that short-range!

I had moved over to the Taliban fighter lying underneath Sep, securing his hands with plastic ties and searching him for any secondary weapons. The compound was now clear, and the detainee was secure. I now identified him as the high-value target we had come to detain. I could now hear helicopters right above us providing overwatch protection. The objective was complete. We had detained the senior Taliban commander from the notorious region of Helmand Province.

It was now time for us to exfil from the compound and walk to the helicopter pick-up point with the detainee before any other Taliban fighters in the immediate area responded to the gunfire and explosions. Leaving by helicopter was always a vulnerable time for the squadron, so we had to move fast! It wouldn't be uncommon for us to spend the night bouncing from target to target, but tonight it was just this one, and we were heading back to base.

There were no hostages to rescue on this occasion. Sep had done his job with excellence. He had protected my life and the lives of my team, proving his name once again, Septicus Maximus.

I was a special forces dog handler in the SAS. My specialist skill was to manage a military working dog on operational deployments worldwide. Sep had been my dog for about a year; after replacing my previous dog, Dackx, who was sadly killed after years of phenomenal service to the Regiment. Dackx had deployed on multiple operational deployments in both Afghanistan and Iraq.

Losing Dackx had cut me deep, and it had taken me a long time to bond with another dog. I held myself responsible for his death for a long time. In the memory of his service to the Regiment, it was an honour that both Dackx and I were selected to be the dog and handler for the SAS 'The Pursuit of Excellence' statue at Stirling Lines Hereford.

Sep and I had been deployed together several times over that year in various locations and roles. Sep wasn't a big dog, relatively short; he made up for what he lacked in size in his bite. He was relentlessly uncompromising in his role, the best working dog I had ever seen.

He had lost most of his tail early in his career and had a very distinct stub that would stick up. It was pretty comical to me on the first day that I took him on as his new handler because Dackx had lost half of one of his ears; I seemed to keep getting dogs with missing body parts.

I remember the first time I walked into Sep's kennel to take him out: he just stood there looking at me and growled, refusing to listen. It took a few attempts to convince him I was his new handler. Sep was an extraordinarily independent and headstrong dog, which proved challenging during our training. Still, it was an incredible experience and a time that I will not forget.

Unbeknown to me at the time, this would be one of Sep's last operational deployments before he would retire after eight years of long hard service in the SAS. Like Dackx, Sep had been on multiple operational deployments in Afghanistan and Iraq. Sep and I were also honoured before he retired, being painted as the dog and handler in a new SAS painting.

It was a huge blessing for me to have both of my boys honoured, one as a SAS remembrance statue and the other in a Regimental Mess painting that will last even beyond my days. Even more surprisingly, I would become Sep's new owner for his final days in retirement, which would end a few years later in South Africa.

Being a dog handler was one of the high points of my career in the special forces. I thoroughly enjoyed it; it was incredibly challenging yet enriching. The best of it was I would always be one of the first ones on the target following the dog, and on every operation, there was always a need for a dog handler, so it was a win-win situation.

I had already mastered several infiltration skills as an operator: walking to an enemy target across an open arid desert, climbing through high mountainous regions barred with snow, or being deep in the humid tropical jungles wading across alligator-infested swamps and rivers.

> ...find the hostages and eliminate any enemy threat that stood in our way.

Walk-in, drive-in, boat-in, or parachute in I now did it with a dog attached to me. No matter what, I had to get the dog onto the target and on time, regardless of the atmospherics we faced or enemy resistance. I had to effectively handle him as he did what he had been trained to do, find the hostages, and eliminate any enemy threat that stood in our way.

Outside of this was his welfare, feeding, medical care, ongoing training and maintenance of readiness. It was all of my responsibility throughout the year, even managing the negative experiences he had so that it would not affect his performance. It was a full-on commitment, not just a pick-up and drop off at the kennel thing; you spent a lot of time together, you had to bond and build trust, and you became family.

Sep

CHAPTER FOUR

A SPECIAL BREED OF MEN

The Special Air Service (SAS) is the world's most elite special forces, formed in 1941 by Captain David Sterling. They were initially known as the Long-Range Desert Group, LRDG. The LRDG mastered desert mobility, developed new desert navigation in the first world war and specialised in airfield raids to destroy enemy aircraft deep behind enemy lines.

Over the next four decades, this special band of brothers would become the global leaders in hostage rescue after the Iranian embassy siege on Princes Gate in South Kensington, London, from the 30th of April to the 5th of May 1980.

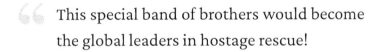

> This special band of brothers would become the global leaders in hostage rescue!

At 11:30 am, six-armed Iranian Arabs took control of the embassy and took twenty-six hostages. The group demanded the release of prisoners in Khuzestan taken during the Arab uprising in the Iranian revolution of 1979.

This hostage situation went on for six days of intense negations between the gunmen and the Metropolitan Police. On the sixth day, they killed a hostage and threw the body out of the embassy.

On the 5th of May 1980, multiple SAS assault teams of men dressed in black overalls wearing respirators and carrying machine guns stormed the building. They abseiled from the rooftop onto these small balconies and then entered through the first-floor windows, followed by several explosions and some gunfire.

Seventeen minutes later, the siege was brought to an end freeing nineteen hostages and killing five of the six terrorists. The remaining gunman served 27 years in prison. For the first time on live television and in front of the world's press, the legendary status of the SAS started.

The years of worldwide campaigns that followed the Iranian Embassy siege would forge an elitist unit, a special breed of man; regardless of the geographic location, conditions, or situation faced, failure was never an option; to a SAS man!

He would die for his brother in the fight to complete the mission and save the lives of the hostages, and it remains that way today. How had this band of brothers forged this way of life?

By an ethos that had become part of them: it was in our blood, a practice we not only operated in but lived by, not something that could be taught or read about in a book. It must be birthed from within the man: self-discipline, humility, and humour, classless but not rankless and most important of all, the unrelenting pursuit of excellence.

> It was in our blood, a practice we not only operated in but lived by...

When you truly receive the revelation of the true meaning of 'the pursuit of excellence.' You will learn that it's never achieved, only a lifetime of the constant pursuit of it as you enhance and perfect every detail of what you do in everything that you do.

The life that came after being badged SAS was worth every moment and all that I had sacrificed. I was always adventurous and enjoyed a challenge. Still, SAS missions took me to new physical and mental limits that I could not possibly imagine.

The impossible circumstances that we would face, with the ever-changing atmospherics on the ground and the fact you walked a very thin line of potentially being killed, or worse, being captured, interrogated and likely tortured, forged my mind.

My focus was always on what was next; operating at this heightened level developed my ability to rapidly think, assess and process the life-threatening conditions we faced and make decisive tactical decisions.

> 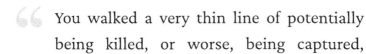 You walked a very thin line of potentially being killed, or worse, being captured, interrogated and likely tortured!

The SAS deepened my ability to strategise and devise complex tactical plans. Our operations would always have multiple layers with vast amounts of detail. Every stage would have several actions for changing the plan as and when the atmospherics on the battlespace changed without the need for discussion within the team; it is what forges an elite unit.

Not every battlefield was the same; My team often found ourselves outmanned and outgunned. We had to fight our way out with no support coming and usually deep into the enemy-occupied territory.

Many battles lasted for hours and some even for days. Fighting in the daylight and then in the dark, in the extreme heat and horrific cold, in the driest remote places known to man, to the wettest amphibious regions on earth, it didn't make any difference as to how we would fight, whatever we faced; we overcame it!

> My team often found ourselves outmanned and outgunned!

Over the years, I had many close calls, from being shot at by sniper fire, bullets landing within feet of where I was standing, to mortars exploding all around me and vehicles being shot at and blown up by improvised explosive devices. It had become quite normal to be shot at by machine gunfire, usually from windows and doorways whilst approaching a target or by rocket-propelled grenades, exploding as they hit the walls behind me and rooftops that I was standing on.

> ...without fear, go 'ALWAYS A LITTLE FURTHER'.

This sphere of operations forged a special breed of man; regardless of the geographic location, conditions, or situation faced, failure was never an option; for a SAS man! He would die for his brother in the fight to complete the mission and save the lives of the hostages, and it remains that way today without fear, go 'ALWAYS A LITTLE FURTHER'.

During my time in the SAS, I developed an extensive range of specialist skills that I had to maintain, always ready to respond or be deployed to a terrorist incident anywhere in the world. Each SAS operator is an expert in operating in any environment, urban, desert, mountain, or jungle. Not only was I a dog handler, but also a sniper and a specialist trauma medic, and over the years in, many other niche skills.

It was paramount that we were always ready to immediately step into any of these roles that required an operator to fulfil the mission. This was our way of life during the intense seasons of warfighting; the war on terror had forged the Regiment into experts in surveillance and close protection.

I had become a close quarter battle instructor training indigenous forces worldwide in both counterterrorism and counterinsurgency. Overtly and in a covert role, many global terrorist networks had become more and more acquainted with hiding themselves within the local population. They were using civilians to cover their movements. Suicide bombers had become their preferred choice of attack against security forces and the civilian population to achieve their aim, to bring chaos and disorder and attempt to destroy government leadership and control. Any opportunity to take a hostage, a journalist, a world aid support or a charity worker was their highest priority: this was now the war on terror.

Our operations were diverse, from deployed to some remote part of the world on a covert surveillance operation, spending weeks or months watching an enemy target to being a part of a close protection team protecting a high-profile figure in a hostile environment. However, being in the SAS, there would always be plenty of action.

From fast-roping onto a rooftop from a helicopter at night to search a terrorist bomb factory to racing speed boats down a jungle river to clear a terrorist training camp, life was never boring in the SAS.

> I was living the dream in the SAS - 'WHO DARES WINS.'

But nothing comes close to jumping out of a plane at night on a hostage rescue mission; I was living the dream in the SAS - 'WHO DARES WINS'.

CHAPTER FIVE
SELECTION

It had been my dream to be a SAS operator, and I had given everything to pursue it. This very pursuit took me years and cost me everything that I had at the time, including nearly my life. It was the most challenging thing I had ever experienced physically, mentally, and emotionally. I had completely underestimated what was required and what it would take to achieve my dream.

Before attempting selection, I completed the Section Commander's Infantry Battle Course at Dering Lines, Brecon, Wales. There were two phases, each lasting three months, the first being skill at arms which trains you how to be a weapons instructor on all infantry weapon systems, and the second phase is tactics, which teaches you how to command a section of men on the battlefield. Section Commanders had prepared me well for the tactical side of selection that I would face, and it had got me extremely fit, and I felt well prepared for SAS selection.

First was the infamous 'Hills' phase over the mountainous regions of the Brecon Beacons in Wales. I remember arriving at the training camp in Wales at the start of selection and there being over two hundred recruits; knowing that only a tiny percentage would pass was quite daunting. I remember thinking that anything could go wrong over the next four weeks, and that would be it. I would be going home; I was on edge after all the preparation and time spent and not knowing what was coming.

Each day for four weeks, I was required to cover distances of over 25 kilometres across the arduous terrain of the Brecon Beacons and against the ever-changing and unpredictable weather conditions we faced. I had to carry my mountain equipment, including my food and water, in my backpack or which, to us, is a 'bergan', which weighed around sixty pounds. Within a week of starting selection, I had begun to pick up injuries throughout my body. A combination of tripping up during tabs and crashing face-first into rocks to the skin burn on my back from running with my bergan, also known as 'bergan rub', I had endless blisters on my feet and black toenails which at some point would fall off, my body had become a bit of a wreck.

Each morning I would wake up at 0400 hrs and start getting ready for the day's march over the hills. It consisted of stretching off the extreme tightness in my leg muscles, straightening my back after sleeping on an old army spring bunk bed, and dealing with delayed onset muscle soreness. Then I would re-tape my feet and do whatever else I needed to do to get my body functioning. At the same time, I would be eating as much as I could whilst drinking a few litres of water to rehydrate; no matter how much I drank, I was constantly dehydrated or bursting for a pee.

As I started to get dressed and get ready to head down to the parade square, the questions would begin to come into my head. What am I doing here? Why am I doing this? Followed by the doubt, Do I want this? Do I need to do this? It wasn't just me; I would listen to the same questions being debated amongst the other lads each night in the psychological battles we faced, and I would witness lads talk themselves off selection and quit.

> The bed spaces in the dormitory became empty by the day.

As the days and weeks went on, the same daily process would become more demanding and monotonous, and the talk in the room got lower and lower as each of us faced his inner mental battle. The bed spaces in the dormitory became empty by the day. During this long month, I had to manage multiple injuries, push through times of sickness, and desperately try to keep my body functioning day after day.

We would drive out into the Brecon Beacons early in the morning to an unknown start point; then, individually, we were sent off on foot on various routes over the

Welsh Mountains. Usually, it was still dark when we set off.

Selection tested my physical fitness and, more importantly, mental resilience and robustness through long periods of isolation and the stress of managing my time, distance, and speed whilst planning my route and analysing the ground both day and night. An instructor would give me my following location as I moved from point to point, known as checkpoints. I would quickly have to assess the ground and calculate the most efficient route to take; wasting as little time as possible and making any mistake in navigation would be costly.

> ...you push your mind and body and go through phases of emotion and pain until you hit your wall where you have to break through it or be defeated.

The final week of 'The Hills' finished with the infamous endurance march of 64 km over the highest features of the Brecon Beacons and all with a 24hr time limit. There are few words to describe what you go through on endurance; after weeks of tabbing before you even start that last twenty-four hours, you push your mind and body and go through phases of emotion and pain until you hit your wall where you have to break through it or be defeated. Nevertheless, I completed endurance after about 18 hours; it was an experience that I will never forget.

Those few of us who passed 'The Hills' went on to do 'The Trees', spending a month in the notorious jungle of Brunei. Going straight from the freezing cold Brecon Beacons into the excessive heat and humidity of the jungle was extreme, causing you to be constantly sweating and fighting dehydration, losing more fluids than you could replace. I lost a vast amount of body weight as I burned more calories than I consumed, let alone carried.

At the time, I remember feeling that this was probably the most physically and mentally challenging thing I had ever experienced at that point in my life, and it took everything from me.

Each day was a fight to stay on my feet and keep moving forward. I was constantly wet from excessive sweating to the heavy jungle rains and frequent crossing through rivers while patrolling. My feet quickly deteriorated, and I grew tired of having to remove leeches from my body. Soldiering in the jungle is the most brutal place in the world as it tests every aspect of your ability to sustain yourself.

The physical exhaustion that the jungle placed on my body due to its terrain and the mental demand of having to operate at this level was just epic. I remember the days thinking if I would be able to get through that day, let alone complete the selection itself.

The jungle is probably the most extreme environment with the most challenging conditions I have faced anywhere in the world; it was foundational to being a tier-one operator within global counterterrorism and counterinsurgency operations. It either broke or made a man, and very few made it to the end.

The small percentage of us who made it through returned to the UK and enjoyed being chased by a hunter force for a week.

This force consisted of over a hundred motivated professional soldiers equipped with night vision and thermal imaging optics. They had search dogs, moved day and night either on foot or in 4x4 off-road vehicles and were supported by helicopters.

 …we were caught and spent a couple of days wearing a sandbag and answering a lot of questions being shouted at us by angry men.

Being on the run with minimal survival equipment and no warm or waterproof clothing was extreme; with no food or water other than what I could find on the ground was a whole new experience that I hope I never have to repeat.

We ran across the mountains and the moors, being chased by this hunter force day and night. Eventually, we were caught and spent a couple of days wearing a sandbag and answering a lot of questions being shouted at us by angry men.

Over the forthcoming months, the few of us left continued with selection and were trained in CQB (close quarter battle) and became experts in hostage rescue.

After six long months of being tested, physically, mentally and emotionally, being set apart from the rest and forged into an elitist, badged and were now SAS.

Selection broke you down and re-built you into something else. It was like nothing you could imagine; most did not make it. No one will ever fully understand until taken to that place.

The instructors on the selection training team were all SAS seasoned operators from the four sabre Squadrons within the Regiment. They led without emotion, giving a very detailed set of instructions at specific times that they expected would be carried out with precision, rarely repeating themselves twice.

Each day would present a new unique challenge which you would have to embrace, overcome, or pack your things up and go home.

I understand now why it takes a SAS man to train a SAS man: you cannot lead someone to a place that you have not been to yourself. Even today, as I write this, I have never met anyone outside of the SAS who understands the limits a man can go.

> 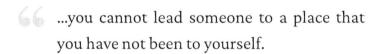 ...you cannot lead someone to a place that you have not been to yourself.

CHAPTER SIX

BORN
A
REBEL

I certainly did not start my life in any way, shape or form as SAS material; I was far from it! I was born in 1979 in the northwest of England. My family lived in social housing during my early childhood in the eighties. At first, my parents had a small two-bedroom flat in a deprived, rundown council area. Many dysfunctional families lived in the neighbourhood, and each day would bring something new.

Properties in the area had their windows and doors boarded up, some as if they were just unoccupied or others because the tenants had smashed them. Many of the boarded-up houses and flats had squatters living in them, with many becoming drug dens and eventually getting set on fire by kids and would be left burnt out; nevertheless, it created places for us to hang out whilst we grew up teenagers.

The area that I had grown up in had a lot of crime which became normal to me; often, you would see people selling drugs, drunks wandering around the streets back and forth to the local pubs, and at times prostitutes walking down the street, or the odd burnt-out shell of a car at the side of the road. Hardly any police would ever come into the neighbourhood unless they came by the dozen to raid a house.

I regularly went home to my mother covered in blood after fighting with kids on the street or being chased by gangs where I had to learn to either escape from them or, when I got surrounded and outnumbered, either fight my way out or suck it up and embrace what came.

My early teens had become a survival ground for what later would be the foundation that I would stand on in joining the British Army and serving in the world's most elite special forces, the SAS.

> I regularly went home to my mother covered in blood after fighting with kids on the street or being chased by gangs...

So, where did all of this begin? I remember waking up at night to loud shouting and swearing; they were the arguments between my parents. My natural father often came home drunk after disappearing for days on end. I would get out of bed and go and stand at the door to my bedroom, looking down the hallway as they argued.

When my mother asked him where he had been, he would lie to her. She knew the truth; neighbours had told her that he had been seen in the pub drunk and going into other women's houses late at night after being at the pub all day. As I stood watching, he became violent with her.

My mother would have bruises and burns on her arms, where my father had stubbed out his cigarettes on her during their fights. Shortly after, my natural father left my mother. I remember it being a tough time as she would always make me dinner and not eat anything herself. I know it was because we had very little money, and she would always go without to ensure I had enough.

She would later meet another man and remarry. My stepfather was a bricklayer by trade, and he provided for us as a family; eventually, we moved out of the council flat that we had been living in and moved into a house.

At eight years old, I became adopted. My mother and stepfather had another three children, making me stepbrother to two sisters and a brother. My stepfather was in and out of work throughout my teenage life. My parents struggled financially for many years and ended up in a lot of debt that they could not pay. Being unable to pay the bills and rent, let alone buy any food, caused many arguments.

After years of struggle, my mother and stepfather lost the house they had mortgaged and found themselves back in social housing and surviving on social benefits. As I became a teenager, I was hanging around in various gangs and often found myself being chased down and beaten by other gangs. I had started to get into a lot of trouble. I was smoking and drinking alcohol, and I would often be brought home by the police.

I became a teenager with a bad attitude, and I just rebelled against my parents and everything they would say. Often it resulted in me being kicked out of the house because I didn't come home on time; I would come home late at night and find the door locked until the next day.

I would frequently get dragged in front of the headmaster during my high school years, usually for fighting. Somehow if there was a fight in school, I was in it. During breaks and lunchtimes, I would leave the school grounds and be off with my mates. We would walk down the railway line tunnels or the local quarry skimming stones on the lake, usually being chased off by security or the police, returning to school late, and getting sent to the headmaster again; it became a vicious cycle.

At one point, I was 14 years old and got drunk with some mates in a local pub and being drunk; we ended up fighting with some other guys who were there. The following week, this lad I had fought with outside the pub had his older brother come to the school looking for me.

At fourteen, I was standing outside the school gate, fighting with this lad's brother, who was about twenty-one years old; this went on until someone in a passing car stopped and got out to split up the fight. Teachers took me to the headmaster; this incident led to my suspension. My parents were strict with me, and their punishment was severe, but I did not care.

My final exams came and went, and I had nothing to show for my school education; I had rebelled against my parents and the teachers in my school. All I wanted to do was join the Army and get away from it all. So I did; I had no idea what I was joining, only that it was the Army and I'd be in the infantry.

The Sergeant in the Army careers office said that I would get fed three times a day, put in free accommodation, and get paid at the end of each month; this sounded great to me! I had been given an official start date and paid my 'Kings shilling', a traditional payment when a soldier signs up to serve in the armed forces. At the time, this was five pounds, which was quite a lot back then.

It was March 1996, I was sixteen years old, and there I was, standing at a train station. I had a small bag containing a few personal items and a rail travel warrant that the Army careers office had given me; it was for a one-way train ticket. I was heading to Scotland to undertake three months of intensive Army training.

I had no idea that I was about to start a journey that would take me around the world to some of the most hostile places known to man, facing life-threatening situations that I could not even imagine.

> 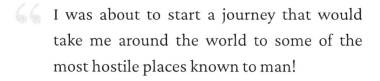 I was about to start a journey that would take me around the world to some of the most hostile places known to man!

CHAPTER SEVEN
ACROSS THE WATER

One of the most obvious things I realised when I started my army training was that I was no longer an individual, no longer a civilian. I had become a unique eight-digit number to identify myself; I was now just a number.

Gradually, our training became harder each week. We would go out on daily marches called tabs for miles over the training area carrying our heavy bergans, helmets, and rifles and spent many weeks out over the vast training areas of the harsh Scottish highlands conducting training exercises learning fieldcraft, tactics and how to administrate ourselves whilst out on patrols for up to several days.

Army training had hit me hard, with the extremely high standards of discipline required, a chain of command with orders to follow, and indeed punishment if you did not adhere. I had found soldiering quite different from anything else that I had previously experienced in my short life.

However, I was good at it; it came naturally to me. I enjoyed the outdoors; the weather conditions did not bother me, and the physical and mental demands that I remember experiencing seemed as if I had already been prepared for it somehow. Eventually, this gruelling long training period ended. Our training was complete; we had an official passing out parade where I received the top student award.

After three months of basic training and three months of specialised infantry training, I was a trained combat soldier. I remember afterwards going on leave, which felt very strange, being back home; everything seemed very different. I could see 'the same people doing the same things' in 'the same places'; nothing seemed to have changed, but I had.

I joined my unit, the Queens Lancashire Regiment, which at the time had deployed on a peacekeeping mission in Bosnia. At eighteen, I deployed to Northern Ireland, known as 'across the water'. The United Kingdom government had been engaged in domestic terrorism with the IRA since 1968. For over 30 years, from the sixties to the late nineties, Northern Ireland experienced severe sectarian violence.

This violent sectarian conflict, called the Northern Ireland Conflict and also referred to as 'The Troubles', had seen 3,600 people killed and more than 30,000 civilians injured. It was rooted in centuries of conflict between the Catholic and Protestant religions.

Ultimately this long conflict was between the Protestant unionists (Loyalists) who desired the province to remain part of the United Kingdom and the Roman

Catholic nationalists (Republicans) who wanted Northern Ireland to become part of the Republic of Ireland. The Royal Ulster Constabulary required ongoing military support from the Ulster Defence Regiment and the British Army during this protracted conflict.

> It was chaos; nothing could have prepared you for it.

Our role in Northern Ireland was simple, to support the Royal Ulster Constabulary, the armed police force of Northern Ireland. Operations were relentless; each day, we would get on helicopters and fly out of Omagh and get dropped off in the countryside of Armagh.

We would then spend several hours patrolling back in, having a brew, and doing it again. Ireland was tough, and I quickly grew up; I remember being sworn at and spat on in the street as I patrolled past civilians. It was chaos; nothing could have prepared you for it.

Don't get me wrong, at first, this was all exciting, but it did not take long before this became a regular occurrence and, in some areas, it became quite dangerous.

We would be shot at in certain areas, from windows or parked cars to even snipers out in the countryside lying in wait. Not to mention the constant threat we faced each day while patrolling IEDs (improvised explosive devices) disguised in what we called street furniture, waiting for our patrols to pass by.

Worst of all was the threat of a car bomb being driven straight at your checkpoint. The driver would have often been under duress; likely, their family would have been taken captive.

There would be regular protests throughout the year where we would have to get dressed in full riot gear with shields and batons. During these protests, it wouldn't take long before they would turn into riots where we would be petrol bombed and bricked. These riots often became hostile and would quickly get out of control, with shop windows getting smashed and then set on fire, and parked cars in the streets would be overturned and set on fire.

During the time I had spent in Northern Ireland, I had witnessed things that changed me! On the 15th of August 1998, I heard a massive explosion just after lunch. There had been a car bomb detonated in the middle of Omagh town, County Tyrone. Later we would find out it had horrifically claimed the lives of 29 people and seriously injured a further 220 people.

The Battalion responded to the incident providing a security cordon around the police dealing with the incident. We assisted with treating casualties and searching for trapped civilians amongst the tons of rubble that went on for the next three days.

The absolute carnage caused to the street was like nothing I had ever seen before. To see so many bodies lying on the floor and many more people just staggering around horrifically injured was shocking. This horrendous bombing attack was by a terrorist group called the Real Irish Republican Army. The images of that day remain etched in my mind; the catastrophic damage caused to human life had changed my whole perspective on terrorism and for what was later to come.

During my second year in Ireland, I was allowed to train as a surveillance operative. I joined a specialist surveillance counter-terrorist unit responsible for maintaining close observations of known terrorists throughout Northern Ireland. This specialist role required me to work closely with Special Branch to develop intelligence and gain evidence of criminal activity for prosecution.

I quickly learned this niche skill, it somehow came quite naturally to me, and it wasn't long before I completed my first commander's course and started to get more and more involved in the planning and leading of our team's patrol operations.

During this time was when I first met members of the SAS. I was fascinated by hearing how the SAS operated and the things that only they could do. I remember when a SAS man walked into the room, it fell silent within a moment, and when they would speak, heads would turn to listen attentively to what they had to say.

As I listened to some of the SAS men talking, it started something within me, a dream of being a member of the elite SAS.

CHAPTER EIGHT
FALLEN WORLD

After my two-year tour of Ireland had finished, I returned across the water to the mainland. I was tired of all that I had experienced during my time there. The physical and mental demand of the last two years had finally taken its toll. Mentally I felt exhausted.

With very little leave during the operational tour combined with the mundane life that we now faced in the Battalion, life was completely different, and we indeed were not the same lads who had left two years earlier. The loss of our operational pay had taken a significant financial impact on me. Everything was adding up, and I felt like I had enough of the Army.

> The skills I had learned in the Army were now paying off big time…

All I could see was my mates back home getting paid a lot more than I was for doing a lot less. They all had flashy cars and went out every weekend enjoying themselves, living a lifestyle I wanted to live whilst I was usually stuck on guard duty most weekends.

So, at the age of 21 years old, after five years of service, I left the Army. Within a week or so of leaving the Army, I had started to apply for jobs, and it wasn't long before I was given one in logistics warehousing and distribution. The skills I had learned in the Army were now paying off big time in this 'new world' that I had entered; it was great. I was earning decent money, a lot more than I had been even whilst deployed on operations in Northern Ireland which I thought was ridiculous, and what's more, I had my weekends off. I quickly learned what to do, and within a few months, I was given more responsibility as a supervisor.

As the months went on and I was making more and more money, it was great, and I felt loaded. I was amazed at how little I had to do for it, plus I had to work fewer hours a day. At last, I was in complete control of my own time and life. I could buy any designer clothes I wanted; I could go out whenever I wanted to and do whatever I wanted; it felt like complete freedom to finally live my life. No one was there to order me around.

I started to go out on Friday nights with mates down to the local pubs and then onto the nightclubs; it was great; I felt like I was now making up for all my lost time. My social life had certainly increased; over time, I started to hang around with some of my old friends that I had grown up with and had not seen since I had joined the Army.

However, things were not quite what they seemed. I had become accustomed to this nightlife. Having developed a considerable number of mates who were always looking to party, it wasn't easy to turn down an invitation to go out. I quickly started to get involved in the wrong circles through friends I knew growing up; this changed everything.

We were into the club scene big time. I'm not talking about high street dance clubs; I'm talking hardcore back street, unlicensed clubs in the worst parts of the city, usually illegal and never stayed open long before they got closed down, but they did have the best DJs at that time. They were full of gangsters and drug dealers; you could not even get in unless you knew the right person. It was common to see someone argue and get bottled sitting at a table or fight on the dance floor where they would get stabbed.

The cost of this lifestyle soon caught up with me; I was spending money I did not have. Did I stop? No! Going out got ridiculously excessive; I would find myself virtually out every night of the week. It got to the point where I was going out on Friday night and staying out until late on a Sunday.

Somehow, I always still found the means to go out; we would consume an absurd amount of alcohol. Spending more and more each time I went out until, eventually, I was spending more than I was earning.

I had begun to use multiple credit cards to facilitate my lifestyle. It wasn't long before I was overdrawn and maxed out on all of my cards. I had got sucked right into the crowd; I wanted to fit in, be accepted and not be left out; it wasn't long before it started taking over my life.

One night, I fought with the security at a nightclub. I remember being grabbed inside the club and dragged outside, I don't remember why, but I remember standing in the street outside the club and going into a rage; I don't know where it came from, but it took over me; I couldn't see or hear anyone. Something inside me drove me to attack the doorman; I just 'went to red' as I charged across the street towards him. I suddenly had enormous strength to take on the security at the door as I grabbed hold of one of them.

> 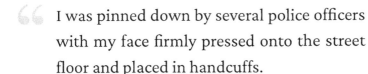 I was pinned down by several police officers with my face firmly pressed onto the street floor and placed in handcuffs.

Moments later, I remember being taken down by a police baton. I was pinned down by several police officers with my face firmly pressed onto the street floor and placed in handcuffs. I was arrested and put into a police van with a police dog and taken to the police station, where I spent the night in a cell. The following week, I stood in the magistrate's court; I did not receive a sentence due to my military service record and operational service in Northern Ireland.

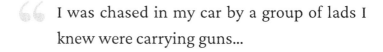

> I was chased in my car by a group of lads I knew were carrying guns...

The people I was associating with had now gained control over my life through my accrued debt. I would end up being involved in arguments and getting threatened with knives in the toilets of clubs. Not having the money, I just avoided their phone calls, but then I would get text messages from them threatening that they were going to break my legs if I did not answer.

Eventually, I was chased in my car by a group of lads I knew would be carrying guns; I was blocked in whist driving down a street and then dragged out of the vehicle and threatened to have my hands chopped off. It was a mental lifestyle.

> ... threatened to have my hands chopped off

I would regularly be involved in fights on a night out merely due to the state of intoxication that I was in, and one particular fight resulted in me getting my head split open and knocked out for about twenty minutes. I came around in the accident and emergency department in a hospital with absolutely no idea where I was or even who I was.

Slowly over the next twenty-four hours, my memory returned, but I couldn't walk for three days due to the extent of the head injury. It took days for me to learn to walk again, my brain told my legs to move, but somehow the message got lost.

Living this way had become so extreme; I could not continue anymore, yet I was in too deep, and the reality was I couldn't get free from it. Each week I would find myself out, again and again, doing the same things with the same people. Something inside me always took over, this wild, uncontrollable part of me taking me over the edge repeatedly as if I was on a mission of self-destruction. So, I just accepted it and went out, again and again, to forget about it.

One night I was at home on my own. I was sitting downstairs when I remember looking at the time. It was around 9 pm, and I just had this feeling that I should go to bed, so I did; strangely, I felt I needed to turn all the lights off and go straight upstairs. Now I never usually did this; anyhow, on this occasion, I did and went and lay down on my bed. I remember lying there; I was nodding off to sleep when I heard a loud boot on my front door; it never opened, followed by heavy thumping on the door and my downstairs window.

I listened to the voices of about five or six men standing outside; then I heard the distinct voice of one of them whom I knew shout through the letterbox. "Kevin, Kevin," he shouted about six or seven times. I knew them, and these lot would have guns on them and shoot someone for a hundred quid. But between my mates, we owed them a lot more.

 God help me, I'm going to die...

As I lay there on the bed, I said, "God help me, I'm going to die; God, please don't let them in...." Five minutes went by, which seemed like a lifetime; my heart was pounding in my chest. Then I heard a car pull up; a few moments later, I heard them talking as they got into the car, the car doors slammed shut, and the car drove away.

 I would 'Go to Red'...

I was unaware that something serious was happening inside me during those years. Anger was gradually building up; this anger would eventually become an inner rage within me; at the click of a finger, I would 'Go to Red' and become uncontrollable. As this developed, it took control of my life. I'd lost my humility and integrity and had no self-discipline in my personal life.

I gradually struggled to suppress it, but it consumed me no matter what I tried. I was embarrassed and couldn't share what I was going through with anyone out of fear of failure or being judged.

I was drastically falling and losing control. I continued to drink excessively and frequently, getting drunk to numb the frustration and eventually, I was arrested for driving over the limit. Once again stood in front of the magistrate's court, but it was not for fighting this time. The outcome, the court's punishment, was a hefty fine and a driving ban.

The following few weeks, I had lost my job, debt collectors had taken my car, and my bank account and all my cards were blocked; I was thousands of pounds in debt, unemployed and banned from driving. I had no choice but to declare myself bankrupt.

I said, "God help me, I don't know what to do...."

In just over three years from leaving the Army, I had managed to destroy my life. As I walked down the street, I said, "God help me, I don't know what to do...."

 I felt so empty inside; I had nothing and no way forward; I was lost.

Everything I had fought for and all that I had achieved was gone, and it was my fault. I had made the decisions that had brought me to this place, and I was responsible and was now facing the consequences. I remember standing in the rain staring at the ground; I felt so empty inside; I had nothing and no way forward; I was lost.

CHAPTER NINE
PIRATES

Over the forthcoming weeks, incredibly, out of nowhere, I received a phone call; an opportunity came up to do maritime security and join a team escorting ships through the Egyptian Suez canal down past Somalia. This had become a lifeline for me to escape from this fallen world I was in.

As I listened to the details of the opportunity being explained and was told it was anti-piracy, I laughed, having the image of a pirate wearing a black patch over his eye and a parrot sitting on his shoulder. However, I soon learned that it was no joke and piracy was real.

The route we would take on the ship forced you through the Gulf of Aden right along the 'Horn of Africa' into the Indian Ocean. As you pass through the Gulf, on one side, you have Yemen, with Al -Qaeda terrorists transiting across the waters into Somalia, heading to the many terrorist training camps or Somalia's rebel group Al-Shabaab crossing into Yemen to support the ongoing war in the middle east.

On the other side was Somalia; you had pirates attempting to seize every ship that would pass by its shores and then take it into Somalian waters to hold it ransom to the ship's insurance companies. Somalian pirates had been seizing ships daily and then demanding millions of dollars in ransom from international insurance companies for their release.

> ...the world's most dangerous water in the world.

During my time in anti-piracy, a band of pirates seized a Ukrainian freighter full of weapons and demanded $25 million for its release. According to some estimates, the insurance companies had paid $150 million to Somalian pirates that year alone. Somalian piracy became a multimillion-dollar enterprise. These pirates were part of a much larger organised crime syndicate directly linked with terrorism; any westerners that may have been on board were also taken hostage and passed through the terrorist network. The Gulf of Aden became the world's most dangerous water in the world.

The Egyptian Suez canal is a shortcut between Asia and Europe. Vital to the global economy for international import-export trade as heading around the west coast of Africa can take almost three times longer, costing three times more. As markets rose and fell overnight, cargo such as oil and gas would lose huge profits before reaching its final discharge destination, often getting re-routed to a more favourable discharge location. Which frequently extended the time that I spent onboard from weeks to months and, at times turning around and heading back the way we had just come, yes, back towards the pirates.

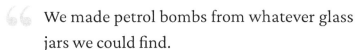
> We made petrol bombs from whatever glass jars we could find.

My team would usually board the ship in Egypt and spend the next two or three days that we had whilst going down the Suez canal to fortify the ship. We would cover the entire perimeter of the ship's freeboard with razor wire and then attach all of the fire hoses to the railings around the ship's deck. Enabling us to turn them on should any small boats come alongside us, creating a spray mist over them, blocking their visibility. We welded all of the doors closed into the ship apart from one door, which we bolted shut from the inside and welded iron bars across all windows, preventing or restricting access to the ship.

Finally, we made petrol bombs from whatever glass jars we could find and put them in crates strategically placed around the ship's deck to defend the ship if attacked as we were not allowed to carry guns, so if that failed, it would be hand to hand using spears if needed. As we approached the coast of Somalia, we would wait, constantly on the lookout day and night for any sign of pirates. At first, I thought it would be unlikely that we would see any pirates; how wrong was I?

 ...past the pirate-infested Somalian waters.

Every day ships were being attacked and taken along that transit corridor; I would listen to the reports coming over the radio of ships in front or behind us coming under attack from pirates. Days later, I would read the messages sent by email outlining all of the ships in Somalian waters under pirate control, recognising some of the names of the ships from hearing them under attack days earlier.

Over the next 12 months, I escorted half a dozen boats in and out of the Gulf of Aden past the pirate-infested Somalian waters, spending around eight months of my life on a ship eating fish heads and white rice. All whilst being chased by small boats, usually packed with pirates firing AK47 machine guns at my ship as they attempted to board us with grappling hooks and ladders.

It was challenging to tell pirates from fishermen until they climbed aboard another boat, pulled out their AK47s, and started shooting at you. Or when their fishing boats suddenly began to race towards you and attempt to block you by firing RPGs (rocket-propelled grenades) at us, exploding just in front of our ship to try to force us to stop so that they could board us and take the ship!

 It was challenging to tell pirates from fishermen until they climbed aboard another boat, pulled out their AK47s, and started shooting at you!

When fishing was not providing for their families, it was not difficult for a fisherman to become a pirate; firstly, getting hold of an AK47 in that part of the world was easy. They already owned a motorboat, so they only needed a ladder or grappling hook and rope to climb on board. Many joined gangs of pirates, placing them in a desperate situation of having no option to take a passing vessel successfully or die trying.

It got to the point I was so sick of the sight of the sea, I was sick of getting smashed by the wind and waves, the horrendous food and I'd had enough of pirates. Fortunately, I got an email at the time, and another opportunity came up for me, which was in Iraq, dry land! I couldn't wait, so I left.

CHAPTER TEN

THE
WILD
WEST

I arrived in Bagdad, Iraq; I was part of a close protection team in one of the wildest places on earth. There were local police checkpoints dotted around the city and out in the desert areas, which we had to pass through each day.

The police were all former militia, untrained and only interested in what they could get from us. Often they refused us passage through the checkpoints and would surround our vehicle, pointing their AK47 machine guns at us. I would spend hours negotiating my way out; we would get shot at whilst approaching the checkpoint on the bad days.

 It was like 'Bandit Country' …

Moving from one area to another, I would encounter different militant groups controlling that area, which could change overnight. It was like 'Bandit Country'; we often spent hours driving around specific areas to avoid the militia groups.

When I think back to those early years in Iraq, when I stayed at the Basra airfield, we got mortared most nights going on through the night. We would sleep in these old rundown portacabins next to the airport's perimeter, so we were in the perfect spot to get hit as it was in the direct line of the airport control tower; at some point during the night, we would hear the mortar attack alarm going off.

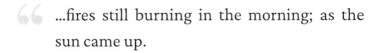
> ...fires still burning in the morning; as the sun came up.

We would have to get out of bed, race to find the nearest bunker, listen to multiple motor rounds being fired and then count them as they randomly land and explode all around us, causing a lot of damage to buildings and vehicles and taking many lives. Some that were fired landed but did not explode and then lay there, able to explode at any time. There would be fires still burning in the morning; as the sun came up, I could see smoke from the various parts of the base that had been hit.

> ...it felt very much like the wild west.

I remember the daily vehicle patrols; we headed out in convoy, and I would constantly anticipate driving into an ambush and having to shoot our way out. Just hoping to keep our vehicle moving, hoping the tyres wouldn't get taken out or that we wouldn't lose engine power if our fuel spilt out. Suddenly, there would be an explosion, and I would see a puff of smoke in my wing mirror from an IED (improvised explosive device) detonating between our convoy vehicles. That time in Iraq was crazy, and it felt very much like the wild west.

 Suddenly, there would be an explosion...

About six months in, I became a team leader for a Medical Emergency Response Team MERT that would be responsible for responding to incidents around Basra. We faced many roadside bombs throughout the city. As time went on, so did the risk; the roadside bombs became more advanced. We started to see an increase in Iranian influence within the terrorist network across Iraq.

Daily, we would see EFPs (explosively formed projectiles) used. These were advanced molten copper warheads fired at your vehicle as you drove through a passive, infer red beam from a house alarm sensor disguised in the rubble at the side of the road. These molten copper warheads would penetrate straight through the vehicle cab or engine block. Many armoured vehicles were ripped in half and burnt out, leaving few survivors; the enemy had become highly effective in their attacks against us.

 Many armoured vehicles were ripped in half and burnt out, leaving few survivors!

Over the two years in Iraq, several of my colleagues got killed in an enemy ambush. It was time for me to leave; over this time, I had a strange conviction to go for SAS selection; I just shunned it at first, but I couldn't stop thinking about it as the months went by.

So I made arrangements to leave Iraq; during my remaining few months, I decided to use the extreme heat to my advantage. I started training, wearing my armoured plate carrier and my daysack filled with ammunition for weight. Each day before and after the mission, I went out and ran around the miles of the perimeter fence of our patrol base.

CHAPTER ELEVEN
THREE YEARS

As I had already left the Army, the only way for me to attempt SAS selection would be to either join back up in the Army and then apply, or join the SAS reserves, complete their reserve selection over a year and then go for regular selection over six months. The advantage of joining the reserves was that it would be the quickest route to go; however, the downside to this would mean I would have to complete two selections which I did and was successful.

> I heard what he said, but it didn't process in my mind; I was speechless.

The following year I was on regular SAS selection, and I completed 'The Hills' and 'The Trees' phases. After returning from Brunei, we each had an interview with the training officer to determine if we would continue with selection. I remember very clearly the day that I went for my interview.

The training officer said, "You have failed to reach the required standard". I heard what he said, but it didn't process in my mind; I was speechless. At that moment, I kept saying in my mind, 'you have failed to meet the required standard' I understood what it meant, yet I couldn't process it.

Something inside me just broke. It's hard to explain it, but after a year-long of preparation and hard training, everything that I had been through, the miles upon miles over the 'Hills' of the Brecon Beacons, the epic month that I had spent in 'The Trees', blood, sweat and tears, my dream of being in the SAS had ended.

The training officer told me that I would be able to return and re-attempt selection. I couldn't believe that I was in this place of complete failure; I hadn't planned to fail, and I hadn't thought about failure. I felt embarrassed that I had failed selection, thinking about my mistakes and analysing everything.

I felt weak because I had failed, and I felt that others would judge me. Shame slowly started to set in. Lots of questions were coming up in my mind. What am I going to do now? What will I tell people when they ask me how I got on? I had to go and collect my equipment and hand it in at the store that afternoon and leave the barracks.

I had given so much, I had spent an enormous amount of time and resources to get to this point, and it all had equated to absolutely nothing. I remember driving out of Hereford and heading home; I thought I couldn't tell anyone; I felt ashamed. Unfortunately, the phone calls started to come in, and I began to get messages from people asking how it went.

Something inside me had changed; something had shifted; I didn't feel as if I was able to start that process all over again. I wasn't even sure whether or not I'd ever have another attempt at SAS selection.

Six months later, I deployed to Afghanistan. On one of our patrols, as we moved through a remote area high up in the mountains, my team came under attack from heavy enemy machine gunfire. During this gun battle with the Taliban, my team moved up a slope to get to high ground to get into the fire support position.

As I got to the top of the hill, I could see an old soviet trench. One by one, my team jumped into the trench, and I was the last one to get in. I took up a firing position with the light machine gun that I was carrying at the time.

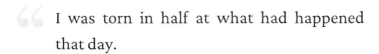 I was torn in half at what had happened that day.

The position was perfect. I could see right down the other side of the hill to where these Taliban fighters had been. I looked directly to my right, and I could see the rest of my team spread out. Within seconds as I stood in the trench, I felt uncomfortable, and I had this indescribable sickness. I felt this intense nausea deep in the pit of my stomach. I felt agitated, followed by frustration and an even deeper feeling of sickness. It was horrendous; I'd never experienced anything like it. I couldn't think of anything other than I had to 'Move'; it didn't make any sense to move; why would I want to move from this position. I couldn't stay there, so I moved my position.

We were engaged in this ongoing gun battle with the Taliban for most of the day and had to call in air support. Sadly, hours after I had moved from the area where I had been initially standing, one of my mates moved down the trench system and passed where I had stood; there had been an IED (improvised explosive device) buried at the bottom of the trench. It exploded, killing him instantly.

That night I sat on the floor in the middle of the desert; there was silence; I sat just staring at the sky; I felt completely numb; I was torn in half at what had happened that day. I've played the events of that day repeatedly in my mind hundreds of times. I struggled with this for over ten years, feeling and thinking that it should have been me; I will never forget that day.

In remembrance of my friend, I took his surname and added it to mine. Over the remainder of the operational tour, I had lost more close friends. We returned from Afghanistan; it was a long dark year for us as we journeyed through this tragic time.

The following year I re-attempted SAS selection for a second time; I completed the 'The Hills' and went to 'The Trees' again. However, after a few weeks in the jungle, I found myself bouncing from one tree to the next during one particular training day whilst patrolling in the intense heat. I passed out with heat exhaustion and hit the floor, and I didn't even see it coming. I was stripped naked by my team, given intravenous fluids, and evacuated by helicopter out of the jungle to the nearest hospital.

My body temperature had gone way above what it could cope with, which was life-threatening. I recovered in hospital, and a few days later, I got sent back to the UK. I went back in front of the training officer again, who told me that this attempt would not count as it was a medical withdrawal and that I would be allowed to have another go at attempting selection. First, I would need to prove that I was fit enough to re-attempt selection to the medical board. I spent the rest of the year training, getting my body back to operating at high temperatures again for prolonged periods.

At the end of that year, I had to go to a specialist disease and tropical testing centre to see if my body could still regulate its temperature safely through sweating. I went into a specialist testing room; I ran on a treadmill for an hour carrying a heavily weighted bergan wearing all of my clothing that I would wear in the jungle, including boots.

Over that hour, the room temperature gradually increased, as did the speed and inclination of the treadmill, all whilst wearing a respirator so that they could measure my respirations. I had a digital thermometer up my bottom, which was not the nicest of tests I've experienced; as you can imagine, I was drenched with sweat and blowing out. After the test, I went to see the doctor.

I remember feeling quite nervous as I sat waiting for him to say that I had failed; I remember watching him go over and over the results checking the information and not saying anything at first. And then, He said that he was amazed that I had passed, with the extent of the heat exhaustion. Given that I had blacked out and my body temperature was so high with the small amount of time that my body had to recover, He said he hadn't seen anyone pass the tests before. The results were not what he had expected; they were completely normal, as if I hadn't had any heat injury, and I had somehow miraculously managed to pass all of the medical tests. The medical board approved me to re-attempt selection for the third time.

It took me three attempts and three years to achieve my dream through failure and near-death, to pass the world's most elite special forces selection, the Special Air Service and get badged 22 SAS. This was the high point of my life; everything I had worked towards culminated in this one moment. Blood, sweat and tears had forged my Regimental blue belt and sandy SAS beret that was handed to me as I stood at the famous regimental clock tower on sterling lines with only a handful of those who had made it to the end.

It was an honour to be a SAS operator, and it was the greatest achievement of my life. I was now living the dream, my dream. During my time in the Regiment, I operated with some of the most incredible lads I've ever met, all from different backgrounds and with different experiences, which started a journey of brotherhood which was tested on the front line time and time again.

However, my time on the Brecon Beacons had not quite finished after a few years in the SAS. I returned to the Brecon Beacons again to do the Platoon Sergeants Battle Course (PSBC). A long three-month gruelling training course that took you beyond your limits as a battlefield commander, leading teams of up to forty men at a time called a platoon. The final ten-day training exercise was extremely arduous. Held over the remote Brecon Beacons, we would have constant engagements with the enemy throughout the day and into the night; this left very little time to do personal admin between the contacts and virtually no time to rest, eating as and when you could. You were either preparing to give orders, actually giving orders or heading out on patrol; once back in, you would do it all again.

Looking back, I remember having around eight hours of sleep during the entire exercise, and that was in blocks of anything between five and twenty minutes long at a time. We were so sleep-deprived that I remember falling asleep standing up, and it was epic.

The final company attack was three days long. I was selected to lead the company as the Regimental Sergeant Major (RSM), which consisted of three platoons; during this time, we remained engaged with the enemy, fighting throughout the day and night as we pressed forward, taking and holding ground.

The PSBC course consisted of over two hundred outstanding professional infantry soldiers, all experienced section commanders with extensive operational experience. I achieved a distinction and an instructor recommendation; it was an incredible honour and privilege to be selected by the training team to be awarded, top student. At graduation, I was presented the famous British Army Infantry bayonet. My name is now written on the wall of honour at the infamous Infantry Battle School Dering Lines Brecon Wales with all the previous top students over the last few decades.

 It took me three attempts and three years to achieve my dream through failure and near-death, to pass the world's most elite special forces selection, the Special Air Service and get badged 22 SAS.

CHAPTER TWELVE
THE NEW FRONT LINE

Over the years in the military, I have deployed to various conflicts worldwide; during this time, I started becoming aware of something sinister that I could see in the enemy we encountered. Coming against some of the most extreme terrorist groups from all over the world, the IRA in Northern Ireland, the Taliban in Afghanistan, Al-Qaeda across the Middle East, Al-Shabaab in Africa and ISIS in Iraq and Syria.

> I was witnessing something dark!

I have seen the enemy's tactics change and evolve over the years in how they would attack us. As time moved on and technology advanced, so did the schemes of the enemy to ultimately degrade and destroy innocent life, drive fear into society, and steal people's liberty. In both overt and covert operations that I deployed on, I started to discern something quite evil that I had not previously noticed. I was witnessing something dark, and it wasn't just another enemy force in a different geographic location; I now could see the same evil working through them all.

> Face to face with terrorist fighters, I could see something, not of this natural world!

My knowledge and skill in natural warfare, tactics and strategy gave me the insight and understanding to see that this enemy had merged itself with the world's civilian population, operating in the shadows to avoid detection. It had become guerilla warfare in the fight against terror. When suicide bombers blow themselves up, this is a red flag we can not ignore. Face to face with terrorist fighters; I could see something, not of this natural world; I now realised the natural enemy that I had been fighting against was demonically oppressed.

I quickly realised that I understood or knew very little about the demonic. Now, let me be transparent with you I was not raised in faith; I was an atheist all of my life; I hated religion, and I had no time for it. I had said on many occasions that God did not exist, and that man had written the Bible to control man. If God existed, then why is the world in such a mess. How could there be so much suffering in the world? I thought it was ridiculous to think of religion as a way to fix these things; to me, God was mythical. I had no interest in churches, priests, or pastors, singing hymns or reading the Bible. I thought it was boring, a waste of my time, and pointless; it seemed almost old-fashioned.

Yet, now I found myself in what appeared to be a debate on good and evil, heaven and hell, light and darkness, so after 37 years, I started questioning my view on if

God existed or not? I had not paid any attention to this before, and I had little knowledge of anything to do with God. For me, 'Life and Death' were quite simple; when you died, you died, and that was it; you were either buried or cremated. I decided that I would be open-minded and neutral in making my own decision; I did not want to be influenced by what other people said or thought.

I was deployed to Iraq for six months, and there was no one I could talk to about this, so after some thought, I did what I felt led to do, go to the only source where I thought I could find the truth: the Bible. Initially, I was ignorant and believed that the Bible was just a book written by the church, so when I learned that it was a collection of sixty-six different books written by about 40 authors over 1500 years. I was astonished and felt foolish that I had judged and discounted the Bible before, as I was not an academic, and I had little understanding of the history of the Bible.

I quickly learned that the Bible is the Word of God; even though it had been written over such a long period by multiple writers, it had one author, God Himself. It is God-breathed, and God speaks directly to all of humanity, every nation, and every generation through its words as they are God's words. Through God's Spirit, the human authors wrote what God wanted them to write, and the result was the perfect and holy word of God. When you read 'The Word of God,' His Spirit confirms the truth of the word within your Spirit; I found it quite fascinating and wanted to experience this for myself, so I thought I would try it and see what happened.

After a few weeks of reading the Bible, I understood that it is divided into two main parts: the Old Testament and the New Testament. The Old Testament is the story of a nation, and the New Testament is the story of a Man. The nation was God's way of bringing the man Jesus Christ into the world, and then Jesus shared the Gospel with humanity.

I had never heard of the Gospel; The word Gospel means 'Good News'. The Gospel is the 'Good News' concerning Jesus Christ and the way of 'Salvation'. So I spent another few weeks reading about the birth, life, death and resurrection of Jesus Christ. I determined that I needed to understand 'Salvation' properly as I believed this was key to gaining the truth on the demonic forces operating within this world, to understand 'Life and Death'.

The first thing I came across was the term 'Sin'. I was unfamiliar with this and had to research it from the beginning 'Creation'. I found out that Satan, 'The Devil,' brought sin to the human race through Adam, the first man. Adam was disobedient to God, so sin entered the human race, and human beings became 'Sinners By Nature.' When Adam sinned, his inner nature was transformed by his sin of 'Rebellion,' bringing 'Spiritual Death' and 'Depravity' to him, which would be passed on to 'All' who came after him. We are sinners not because we sin; we sin because 'We Are Sinners'. This passed-on depravity is known as 'Inherited Sin.' Just as we inherit physical characteristics from our parents, we inherit our sinful natures from Adam.'

> ...the punishment for sin is death, spiritual death, which is 'Separation from God,' the Source of all life.

I learned that since that time, sin had been passed down through 'All The Generations Of Humanity,' and we, Adam's descendants, have inherited sin from him, so 'Death' was passed on to 'All Men' because the 'Wages Of Sin Is Death.' The penalty for this sin is death, not just physical death but eternal death. Regardless of your view on good and evil, right or wrong, we have all sinned against God, and the punishment for sin is death, spiritual death, which is 'Separation from God,' the Source of all life.

I read the Gospel, and it said that God so loved the world that He sent His one and only Son, Jesus Christ, who was, in fact, God himself, into the world as a man to put right what we could not do ourselves. The Son was already in heaven, but He was willing to leave; He left his Father and became a man. Jesus died on a cross, and His blood paid the price for our sins to redeem us back to God; Jesus was buried in a tomb and delivered over to death, and on the third day, Jesus rose from death, conquering all sin and its penalty, 'Eternal Death.'

The Scriptures clearly explained to me that the Gospel is the power of God that brings the gift of 'Salvation' to whoever 'Believes.' We cannot earn our salvation; the work of 'Redemption' and 'Justification' is complete, having been finished on the cross. We were once enemies of God in rebellion and have now been 'Reconciled by the Blood of Jesus Christ.' We are adopted into the family of God as there is no condemnation for those who are in Jesus Christ.

I then realised from reading this that it was clear that to reject the Gospel is a lack of faith in the Son of God, God's only 'Provision for Salvation.' God did not send his Son into the world to condemn the world but to save the world through him. Whoever believes in him is not condemned, but whoever does not believe stands condemned already because they have not believed in the name of God's One and only Son.

> 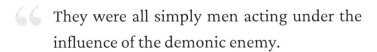 They were all simply men acting under the influence of the demonic enemy.

I had now realised that this demonic influence through the various terrorist groups had been the same enemy, a dark generational demonic force that used man to fight against man since the age of man. Throughout history, you can see clearly, every dictator who has risen. Every holocaust, every act of genocide that has taken place. The nations where a people have been taken into slavery overnight. Human trafficking for-profit, Islamic extreme terrorist groups, every conflict every war was a portal to evil. They were all simply men acting under the influence of the demonic enemy.

I had witnessed some severe demonic manifestations; I had questions that I could not ignore; I needed answers; I knew it was evil, dark, and like a death that I had not seen before. I was standing on this ancient battlefield forged since man's creation and fall, thousands of years of enemy possession, oppression and slavery, principalities over nations, and influence within the deceived lost church.

> I was standing on this ancient battlefield forged since man's creation and fall.

Like any operation in the special forces, we would carry out surveillance on the enemy target to gain intelligence to strategise a course of action to take on how to approach the enemy target to infiltrate and overcome it. We would then form a plan and execute it, taking action when the atmospherics changed. Over these next three months, this would be my approach and posture in pursuing the truth of the existence of a living god.

> I realised everything He said was about death to life, darkness to light, and all about the enemy.

Throughout my time in the Army, whenever we would write reports on the enemy, we always wrote it in red ink; this was so that it stood out from the vast amount of information. You could go straight to it as this was crucial information and probably the most important to know.

As I started to read the Bible, I discovered that the words that Jesus spoke whilst He was in the world are also written in red, and what's more, I realised everything that He said was about death to life, darkness to light, all about the enemy. I had to go deeper; I had to press in to find the truth about this new enemy I had encountered.

> ...the words that Jesus spoke whilst He was in the world are also red.

I learned how the demonic influenced humans, and I now saw that influence in my own life. I have always come against doubt and discouragement from others and myself. For example;

'It's not going to work, and you're not going to make it. Give up now why you can. You're on your own, and no one else cares. You're going to fail; You will get laughed at. Don't embarrass yourself. You should be ashamed of yourself. Why try again? Don't bother. You are wasting your time. You are weak and sick, and you won't recover. You don't need to do this; no one will understand you. People don't care what you think. No one wants to listen to what you say. Nothing is going to change. You're stuck. It's too difficult; why waste your time? You are going to struggle, and no one will help you. You have failed before you will fail again. Have another drink, treat yourself; why not have another? It doesn't matter about the money, don't worry about it, have fun, do what you want to do, don't care about other people or what they think, look after yourself and have what you know you need to make yourself feel better, worry about it tomorrow.'

It's absolute chaos when you find yourself in this place, and I'm sure you can relate to this turbulence of thoughts bouncing around our awareness. I always paid these thoughts attention; I was affected by them, I often spent hours thinking about them, usually late at night in bed, and I couldn't sleep. I felt frustrated; it caused anxiety and, ultimately, stress. I thought to myself, well, I suppose it's because I'm analysing it all to figure out a solution to the problem to make the right decision. I assumed that because of my experience in the Army, I just had a hyperactive mind and over-thought things because of my training.

> ...they were a demonic influence suppressing my life like an enemy machine gun would do during a gunfight.

But the reality was that this mindset and thought pattern in my life adversely affected my life and relationship with others. What's more, it was all of the time; I could not shut it down. Let me be clear this has been something I've had my whole life, growing up, before the SAS, whilst I was on selection for the SAS, during my time in the SAS. The only time these voices quietened was when I obeyed them; when I didn't, they got louder and louder and wouldn't stop until I did. Where did they come from?

> I was pinned down by a demon sniper in the trenches...

They were wicked; they were a demonic influence suppressing my life like an enemy machine gun would do during a gunfight. I had been under enemy fire for years without even knowing; I was getting hit repeatedly; I had demons watching my life and speaking lies into my mind to steal, kill, and destroy me. I was pinned down by a demon sniper in the trenches with nowhere to move to and no air support to call in; this was **'The New Front Line!'**

CHAPTER THIRTEEN
STRONGHOLDS

F or the last 37 years, I could see how the enemy was trying to destroy my life by leading me on a path of self-destruction, manipulating me, deceiving me, and tempting me to do evil things and live in the darkness. I had spent years listening to the voices of doubt, the whispers of discouragement and condemnation coming from somewhere deep within me.

I thought and believed they were my thoughts whilst it was the enemy's schemes against me to destroy my life: All of these thoughts had one common denominator - they had no encouragement, affirmation, or edification. I discovered that they were all rooted in something very dark, and I could now see that these thoughts were not my thoughts. They had a different source, rooted somewhere else that was not me.

I now realised at this point, also how the enemy could easily influence those close to you in how they would respond or behave with you to the very things that they would say. I quickly realised the ability to discern the root of the source of the thought was critical before holding on to it.

I realised the importance of keeping a small circle of influence around you of trusted people who you permit to advise you in difficult times. People speaking into your life is crucial, but be aware that not everyone who appears to be doing well or doing the perceived right thing is in a place to speak into your life either.

Many are raised to positions of power and influence over people. They are often celebrated and cheered on without the understanding or realisation that they are indeed under strongholds themselves and very much under demonic oppression and influence.

I spent three months doing my research; I didn't find this out through anyone else; I read about it and spent time contemplating what I had read as it spoke to me about what I experienced during this time. Spending time in God's Word brought me new revelation, and I believe God showed me that I had generational strongholds in my life and that I was in bondage. I had inherited them from my natural father and him from his and likely so on down my bloodline.

 I had generational strongholds in my life!

I had spent enough time taking down enemy strongholds in Afghanistan and Iraq in my time in the SAS, kicking my way through doors or blowing them in on an enemy target. The 'natural' enemy strongholds I had experienced were always dark, cold, and felt eerie. The terrorists' behaviour that I encountered was not normal; they almost seemed as if they were possessed in an unlike human manner, which I could now see was because of their connections to a spiritual enemy operating through and in them.

> ...alcoholism, addiction, promiscuity and profound violence that birthed a rage within me.

However, I never thought that I had demonic strongholds in my life that were generational from my natural father. The strongholds that God showed me were alcoholism, addiction, promiscuity and profound violence that birthed a rage within me.

These strongholds were rooted deep within my soul, controlling and influencing my mind and emotions. It has defined my character and behaviour and affected all of my decisions in life; I had no love, peace or joy in my life, the things of God; in fact, what I did have was frustration, anxiety, stress and fear; the things of the devil.

Through the Word of God and the discernment, I had received. God showed me how the devil and his demons had taken me on a path of 'self-destruction.' They would lead me to 'Eternal Death' in hell if they were not dealt with, and they needed to be taken down permanently removed from my life.

> 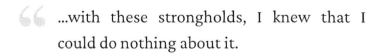 ...with these strongholds, I knew that I could do nothing about it.

At that moment, a realisation hit me straight in the face, and I felt sick to my core. I knew that these strongholds would come over my marriage and my children and my children's children.

I knew warfare well I had spent my life becoming a special forces operator in the world's most elite unit. I had raided well-defended enemy targets worldwide, fortified enemy compounds in the desert with multiple machine-gun bunkers, and I knew what it took to take those strongholds down, but with these strongholds.

I knew that I could do nothing about it; I was utterly devastated to learn this truth and the implications for my life and future; it broke my heart to feel so helpless.

CHAPTER FOURTEEN
SEVEN DEVILS PART 1

As I learned more about the nature of demonic strongholds, I discovered their foundation in our mind is connected to our Spirit through our soul, involving our intellect, emotions, and memories all being used against us. Our Spirit is ultimately suppressed and unable to do anything; under oppression, our soul takes over, which is bondage. Therefore, we cannot come against the stronghold. So all of our desires are always met regardless of what they are.

I discovered that small windows are created through the temptation of that evil desire within us to sin when we give it attention. This weakness is like a window on a physical stronghold; it is its weak point. We would always abseil from the rooftop, down to the window, blow the window in, and go through it to clear an enemy stronghold. The more attention we give to the window (a window of opportunity), we offer for the enemy to come against us.

> Small windows are created through the temptation of that evil desire within us!

As we decide to pursue that temptation (the window) and engage with it, it becomes a door. It is now fully open, giving access to demonic influence. This was no different to us during our operations. We looked for windows and doorways on the target to blow through to gain entry into an enemy stronghold.

We turned a window into the primary way in and out of that stronghold; it became our doorway. The enemy looks for the same to come through into our lives, turning a window of opportunity of temptation into the main door of access to influence us and oppress us.

> ...demons operating under the satanic rule came through like the militia.

I slowly learned to identify the demons moving through the doorways that I had opened to them; the strongholds over my life that held me in bondage intensified the demonic activity in my life.

These demons operating under the satanic rule came through like the militia groups I was surrounded by in Iraq. They swarmed into areas of my life to oppress me, none of them directly in control but all under a higher authority, each with a demonic assignment against a specific area of my life, to steal, kill, and destroy.

> I slowly learned to identify the demons moving through the doorways that I had opened to them!

THE SEVEN DEVILS

It was now evident that there is a demonic hierarchy, a principality with a higher power where there is order and control of these demons in this realm of darkness.

I now identified how they manifested themselves through the doorways that I had created in my life through agreement, allowing them to influence my thoughts through subtle suggestions camouflaged as my own.

It was like the most dangerous waters in the world, an organised, well-executed pirate attack on my mind. I identified their influence and oppression as follows;

The Devil of Distraction: Overload you with different sources of information to take your attention away from God.

The Devil of Disruption: Overwhelm you with confusion and chaos in your life to prevent you from thinking about God.

The Devil of Domination: Increasing the temptation of your desires, turning your attention away from God.

The Devil of Degradation: Degrade your mind causing misery, birthing anxiety, fear and doubt in God.

The Devil of Division: Bring disunity in your relationships, create mistrust and encourage judgment of others and unforgiveness; hardening your heart towards God.

The Devil of Deception: Deceive you from the truth, convincing you that what comes from the world is true, encouraging complacency, justifying compromise in your life leading to corruption, creating idolatry and rebellion to undermine God.

The Devil of Delay: Delay you from believing in God's existence, convincing you to think about it tomorrow.

CHAPTER FOURTEEN
SEVEN DEVILS PART 2

God started to reveal doorways that I had created during my life and how they allowed demonic influence and oppression. I discovered that these doors were a channel for a way in; how did they get there? I put them there through bad, immoral choices and sinful behaviour.

Things that I watched and listened to, most of which I had become morally compromised and corrupted, daily engagement in these things made me complacent and hardened my heart; as a result, I accepted them and justified them in my life.

How did the demons come through? Listening to their lies and their deceit and agreeing with them permitted them to come into my life and take complete control of it; I lived in the darkness through their evil influence, and I allowed them in by agreeing with them to do what they wanted to do and often being entertained, satisfied and pleasured by it; it was through the power of agreement. . Throughout my life, all of the choices I've made and things that I've done, the violence, sexual immorality, excessive alcohol, and drugs, I had opened up some severe demonic doors to the enemy that I never realised was possible.

> 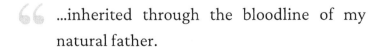 ...inherited through the bloodline of my natural father.

On top of the generational strongholds that I inherited through the bloodline of my natural father, it destroyed my life for years, and I was completely unaware. This revelation opens your eyes to what's going on in the world. It makes you understand then that there are people with significant financial power and influence who also have strongholds in their lives and are clearly directly influenced by the demonic.

Did they get to where they are themselves, or did the enemy lead them there, raising them in places of power and influence to then use their influence to destroy humanity? I now understood the works of the devil and his demons. They have been watching humanity for thousands of years. They know our human ways well, seeing all of our weaknesses successfully tempting man to do evil, leading him to his eternal darkness and death in hell. It was like fighting the Taliban, seasoned terrorists who knew the ground they fought on and the people they terrorised. Like the Al- Shabaab networked through Africa, operating through the corruption of power and influence of a nation.

> I had so much regret and guilt in my life that I was drenched in shame.

After so many years of fighting the enemy, I realised that this enemy had to be dealt with differently to take these kinds of 'strongholds' down. So I started to talk to God; I knew from what I had read in the Word of God that I was talking to Jesus. At first, I felt stupid; however, this was important to me, so I began to do this daily when I was out running as this felt the most comfortable to me, and I just said what I thought. It wasn't pretty; what I said was very bold, and probably it didn't seem to make much sense if you had been listening to our conversation.

I was baffled by many things going on in my life; I had lots of questions about what He had been showing me in His word and revealing to me; one question created another and then another. It was very erratic; the conversation was all over the place; I lost track of what I had been saying over the days and probably got myself more confused.

I quickly learned that you don't always get answers straight away, and God doesn't always answer all of your questions; I was highly impatient with Him; one day, I got so frustrated, I was shouting at Him, blaming Him and basically, I gave up. I ignored Him for a few days and then tried again. One of the biggest things I struggled with within our conversations was my feelings about my sin. I had so much regret and guilt in my life that I was drenched in shame. I felt embarrassed and condemned. I could not understand that His blood washes us clean because of His atonement; it purifies us over every sickness, mind, body, and soul.

> I was a SAS operator, and the enemy had deceived me.

Yet I felt condemned; I felt unworthy about what I had done in my life; what I had done to Jesus after what He had done for me on the cross was irreparable and could never be put right. I still had an onslaught of thoughts of discouragement and doubt that I realised as I had gone on this journey of discovering truth for myself had increased. Now that I was attempting to speak to God about how I felt and what I was going through, these whispers, these lies became darker and very sick accusations, and I struggled to overcome them. They wore me down; they made me emotionally numb.

> ...this smokescreen used against me was by the devil.

God showed me heavenly images to understand the opposite of what I was experiencing in this life. It was an inheritance to come for those who believed. This revelation and understanding broke through the arrogance, ignorance, and pride I had been bound to. Completely unaware of it, how had I been so blind. God showed me that I had been so distracted by the things of this world. God's three gifts had been taken out of my hands and used against me, the gift of life, the gift of time and most importantly, the gift of free will.

They had become like a smokescreen I would use to move past the enemy without being seen, but this smokescreen used against me was by the devil. The enemy's defences were simply layers upon layers of lies to take my eyes off Jesus. I was a SAS operator, and the enemy had deceived me.

I had a vision of hell; it was not what I had thought it would be like; what I felt was a constant internal torment of separation from life; there was no fire as we see in movies; it was absolute darkness without light. I was blind as I had no sight anymore, no longer having a body; it was colder than anything I had ever experienced. God is the source of all life, and eternal death is separation from Him. I was shocked to see that there were also believers in hell who had turned away from Jesus and chose to live in rebellion against Him.

 Eternal death is separation from Him!

CHAPTER FIFTEEN

WHAT IS TRUTH PART 1

Throughout the months I spent deployed in Iraq, I intentionally started to pursue God to find out the truth for myself. At first, I was extremely self-conscious, preventing me from focusing on God; I was frustrated, anxious, and highly impatient, preventing me from thinking of anything other than what I was thinking and how I felt. Whilst I was out running and talking to God, I started listening to some worship music to try to understand what the lyrics meant.

> 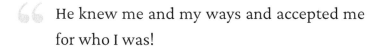 He knew me and my ways and accepted me for who I was!

I would sit somewhere outside at sunrise or sunset, on my own, looking out into the desert and talking about all kinds of stuff. I would ask lots of different questions and then usually forget what I had said, have awkward moments of silence, and feel stupid for even trying. Then I would get up and walk off and give up; there were times I got angry with God, shouted at him and blamed him for the mess I was in, the mess that I had got myself in, and then I walked off and gave up.

A few days later, I came back and tried again; it was good to learn later that this didn't phase God; He knew me and my ways and accepted me for who I was and where I was in my life.

I started to take my eyes off myself and my needs; I put them on God and patiently waited. I genuinely wanted to encounter Him; I would begin to experience God's presence, the atmosphere in the room would change, and I would physically feel His presence. I initially had the understanding that God may or may not turn up as He could be somewhere else. Until He showed me that I did not have to wait for Him because He was already there in the room and had never left; He was everywhere at once, God is omnipresent, meaning in all places, so He has always watched me since birth. I was in the middle of nowhere, deep in the deserts of Iraq, sitting on my own in a portacabin surrounded by razor wire, sandbags and concrete T-walls, and God met me there.

He came precisely to where I was in the world, 'a desert' and not only that, but God came down to where I was mentally and emotionally confused and lost so that I could engage in conversation and understand Him at my level in an experiential way.

As I continued, it helped me accept in my mind that God is omniscient, which means all-knowing, meaning God knows everything; I then realised He knows every detail, every thought, and feeling I had ever had. He knew me better than I knew myself. And of course, at this point, there was no denying God is omnipotent, meaning all-powerful. He is the creator.

 He knew me better than I knew myself!

I now had received the revelation of eternity; I no longer just had thoughts about natural life and death. I was now consumed all the time with thoughts about my eternal life and death and the consequences. Eternity now seemed more real than my life in this temporal world, and many things I valued had lost value. God was not in eternity somewhere; He is eternity, and we are in Him.

I started to realise that one of the obstacles that got in my way when I was trying to spend time with God was that I did not feel that I would be accepted. Honestly, I felt ashamed of my past, embarrassed of the decisions I had made in my life, the things that I had wasted, and the things I had done to others in my selfishness and prideful unforgiveness. I thought it would be impossible to receive forgiveness from my Heavenly Father.

I realised the moment I started to feel His presence of how accepted I was by Him no matter what I had done in my life; I felt His unconditional love. I felt accepted as a son. He would speak, but one word into my being and everything would change, hundreds of questions answered, and a hundred more new ones would come in just a moment.

A real hunger started to grow in me, a genuine, authentic desire in my heart to spend more and more time with Him and get to know Him more; why wouldn't I? He was my creator, my heavenly Father, and it would have been pretty weird, in fact, evil if I had not wanted to spend time with Him; I had made enough mistakes in my life, and this was not going to be one of them.

> He would speak, but one word into my being and everything would change!

These last three months that I had spent pursuing God were not based on a theoretical relationship. It was an experiential relationship in private between God and me and looked nothing like any religion that I had ever seen or would have expected because there was nothing to compare it to. I just had to speak to Him by faith as if I was talking to my earthly father; I now talked to my 'Heavenly Father.' God spoke words deep inside of me, things that I needed to hear in a way that He knew I needed to hear them, and it made me realise He's a loving Heavenly Father.

Let me tell you; He is with you right now! He is patiently waiting for you to talk to Him about your feelings. What is on your mind because He cares about you and what you are going through. Still, you have to invite Him into your life and give Him permission to move through you and do what only He can do.

Only when I silenced the noise in my mind could I hear God's still small voice deep within me. In some of my conversations, I realised that I did not have to negotiate with God to get time with Him; He is always available; I also learned that I don't need to do anything to get His attention; I always had it. I was the one who put Him to one side and took my attention off Him; it was a total transformation of my mind to realise this truth; how had I not known any of this before? Why had nobody told me this?

> 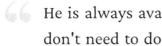 He is always available; I also learned that I don't need to do anything to get His attention; I always had it!

God led me to scriptures to read; They were the words of Jesus Himself that He spoke when He was in the world; at first, I found it difficult to read them. I was reading them too quickly, and I was reading pages; it confused me, and I got frustrated, but I felt led to read only a sentence or two and spend time talking to God about what I had read. As I read them, the words on the paper came alive; the truth penetrated my heart.

I suddenly realised this was no ordinary book. Sure it was words on paper in a book in the natural world, but in fact, it was 'God's Living Word' supernaturally brought to life by God's Spirit; now I could see it clearly; I now knew that you needed the author present; it's not just some book to race through; it's not about gaining knowledge. It's about the truth revealed to us through God's Holy Spirit here with us on earth; if we are willing to hear, He will open our eyes.

These are the scriptures that I read which changed everything for me as the truth was revealed to me by God's Spirit as I read them slowly over time as I spoke to Jesus. I have included them in this book so that you may also read them and hear the truth; Jesus will reveal the truth of them Himself to you.

THE WORD BECAME FLESH

THE WORD BECAME FLESH

In the beginning, was the Word, and the Word was with God, and the Word was God. He was in the beginning with God.

All things were made through him, and without him was not anything made that was made. In him was life, and the life was the light of men.

The light shines in the darkness, and the darkness has not overcome it.

John 1:1-5 ESV

YOU
MUST
BE
BORN
AGAIN

YOU MUST BE BORN AGAIN

Now there was a man of the Pharisees named Nicodemus, a ruler of the Jews.

This man came to Jesus by night and said to him, "Rabbi, we know that you are a teacher come from God, for no one can do these signs that you do unless God is with him."

Jesus answered him, "Truly, truly, I say to you, unless one is born again, he cannot see the kingdom of God." Nicodemus said to him, "How can a man be born when he is old? Can he enter a second time into his mother's womb and be born?"

Jesus answered, "Truly, truly, I say to you, unless one is born of water and the Spirit, he cannot enter the kingdom of God. That which is born of the flesh is flesh, and that which is born of the Spirit is Spirit. Do not marvel that I said to you, 'You must be born again.' The wind blows where it wishes, and you hear its sound, but you do not know where it comes from or where it goes. So it is with everyone who is born of the Spirit."

Nicodemus said to him, "How can these things be?"

Jesus answered him, "Are you the teacher of Israel and yet you do not understand these things? Truly, truly, I say to you, we speak of what we know and bear witness to what we have seen, but you do not receive our testimony. If I have told you earthly things and you do not believe, how can you believe if I tell you heavenly things? No one has ascended into heaven except he who descended from Heaven, the Son of Man. And as Moses lifted up the serpent in the wilderness, so must the Son of Man be lifted up, that whoever believes in him may have eternal life."

JOHN 3: 1-15 ESV

FOR GOD SO LOVED THE WORLD

FOR GOD SO LOVED THE WORLD

"For God so loved the world, that he gave his only Son, that whoever believes in him should not perish but have eternal life. For God did not send his Son into the world to condemn the world, but in order that the world might be saved through him.

Whoever believes in him is not condemned, but whoever does not believe is condemned already because he has not believed in the name of the only Son of God. And this is the judgment: the light has come into the world, and people loved the darkness rather than the light because their works were evil.

For everyone who does wicked things hates the light and does not come to the light, lest his works should be exposed. But whoever does what is true comes to the light, so that it may be clearly seen that his works have been carried out in God."

JOHN 3: 16-21 ESV

THE AUTHORITY OF THE SON

THE AUTHORITY OF THE SON

"Truly, truly, I say to you, whoever hears my word and believes him who sent me has eternal life. He does not come into judgment but has passed from death to life."

JOHN 5:24 ESV

I
AM
THE
LIGHT
OF
THE
WORLD

I AM THE LIGHT OF THE WORLD

Again Jesus spoke to them, saying, "I am the light of the world. Whoever follows me will not walk in darkness but will have the light of life."

JOHN 8:12 ESV

CHAPTER FIFTEEN

WHAT IS TRUTH PART 2

I realised that God's Son, Jesus Christ, existed before creation and that Jesus is the Word of God. Jesus is light, and light is God's eternal life. Death is living in darkness, the opposite of God. I could see that I would never enter heaven; I knew that I would never see heaven, let alone stand at its gates trying to look for an opportunity to negotiate my way in; there would be no second chances to try to justify my decisions and actions.

I now understood the meaning of the Spirit by the wind and now knew that it's 'GOD'S SPIRIT IN YOU' that brings you from 'DEATH TO LIFE' when you are 'BORN AGAIN' to enter God's Kingdom. I now knew that it was impossible to take any darkness or death inside God's Kingdom as there is no sin, no evil in heaven.

Jesus Christ is the Saviour of the world, and He has expounded in all the Scriptures the things concerning Himself and the Divine plan for man's redemption. Such as "Fear not, I am the first and the last, and the living one. I died, and behold, I am alive forevermore, and I have the keys of Death and Hades. Write, therefore, the things that you have seen, those that are and those that are to take place after this" Revelation 1:17-19 ESV.

Jesus led me out of the darkness and into the light as I started to believe in Him.

I knew I could receive salvation and be 'Born Again' regardless of my past, and God would wipe everything away. Including taking down the strongholds over my life; I had no reason not to want to receive this; why would I not want to spend eternity with my Father in Heaven?

The very thought is evil and demonic, and I would be deceived if I thought otherwise after hearing this truth. The moment I read this, I knew that Jesus was the WAY to eternal life. Jesus led me out of the darkness and into the light as I started to believe in Him.

I now had a conviction that I knew that Jesus was the TRUTH, and I knew that I believed by my Spirit, not my mind. From reading these scriptures with an authentic desire for truth and spending time talking to Jesus, I knew that His Word was the truth. It was my free will that He had given me to choose to turn away from my sin and turn to Jesus, to be willing to move out of the darkness and into the light, that Jesus was the only way to life.

Understanding why when we become 'Born Again', we do not just leave the world and go straight to our eternity in heaven to be with God, it was made clear; God explains that we must be formed into the image of his Son, Jesus, who is the firstborn of many sons.

We are the kingdom of God as we carry it within us, our Spirit immersed in His Spirit living within us; we are a living Holy Temple of God advancing the kingdom of heaven forward against all darkness. We carry the light within us, the truth, to take back what was lost, and the gates of hell shall not prevail.

Our lives here as children of God prepare us for appointments in heaven's council and rulership of things we could not possibly imagine. What we see created in the natural, how much more has God created in the supernatural? We must learn here and demonstrate our faithfulness to be trusted with much more.

One day I heard the whisper of God in my Spirit speaking to me. Jesus showed me how He prepares a table in front of our enemies and how we receive righteousness from God's bloodline shed on the cross so that we may cross over the bridge between heaven and earth. It was through Him.

God does not see our sin; He sees our character in His Son, Jesus Christ. This truth made me remember what I had read in the Gospel about when we believe we are born again, set free from bondage; the bondage I had was these strongholds in my life, overrun with demonic oppression.

I now realised why I had avoided talking to anyone about whether I believed God existed or not. The fear of being judged for so long. I felt that my past condemned me because of my regret and shame. I knew now that I needed the blood of Jesus over me. But I then realised I was not born again.

I was living in darkness; my free will kept me in bondage. I had kept myself in the dark, living in sin, and I had been unwilling to come into the light out of fear of the complacency, compromise and corruption in my life exposed before God.

God had given me free will. I realised that free will does not mean doing anything that I wanted to do, as I have physical limitations, but the ability to choose whatever I want within the bounds of my physical limitations. I now realised that I had freely chosen to disobey God, and I was free to determine ways to disobey God because that is what I wanted to do.

I abused my gift of free will for my selfish desires and decided to sin against God. He honours our free will and will not force Himself on us. You have to invite Him and permit Him to work in you.

At 37 years old, my eyes opened, and I heard the truth, and the truth set me free.

I have spent more time in darkness than I have in the light. I wanted to step out of the darkness and into the light and live my life in truth. I did not feel any life in me; I thought I was a failure; I felt weak; I had so much regret and embarrassment, shame and condemnation. It was a path of self-destruction leading me to death.

At 37 years old, my eyes opened, and I heard the truth, and the truth set me free. The voice of my creator, the living God, told me that He sent His one and only Son into this sinful, fallen world for me as the man Jesus who is God Himself. Jesus left heaven, left his Heavenly Father and was born as a human who lived His life free from sin. Rejected, brutally beaten, stoned.

Jesus tied and bound by His wrists to a post in front of all to see. He was whipped to near death by soldiers with leather and metal spikes, tearing His flesh in stripes from off His back; the spikes punctured His lungs, and He could hardly breathe; Jesus collapsed onto both of His knees in unimaginable pain, covered in His blood, by His stripes I am healed.

After this horrific torture, drenched in blood, sweat, and tears, He staggered, barely able to walk. Falling over time and time, He carried His cross in the extreme heat of the day through an angry, violent crowd as they abused Him, mocked Him, through rocks hitting gashing His head open, and spat in God's one and only Son's face. He had not eaten or had any water for days, beyond what I know is possible.

He staggered step by step, crushed by a heavy tree pressing down onto His punctured lungs, filling with His precious blood for me so I may breathe. He knew that the cross was waiting for Him, and that was the only way He could save me from death. He did this for me, my children and my children's children.

Jesus' heart was torn in half; He knew everyone who rejected Him because He made them, watching them be born into the world and grow up as a child; He loved them unconditionally. Jesus was nailed to the cross through His hands and feet and raised up high into the scorching sun for all to see.

The sky became dark as Jesus hung on that cross; physically, mentally and emotionally, He was exhausted more than anything I can imagine or have ever experienced.

He could see hell's demons laughing at Him as they surrounded Him, ready to take Him. The devil stood smiling, thinking he had now won by killing God's only Son; the cheers from hades were like a roar.

With the sins of the world directly placed on Jesus, the darkness was now covering the light. All evil and wickedness of man were on Him, and at that moment, His Heavenly Father, whom He loved so very much, turned His face away from His one and only Son, Jesus Christ, as He could not look at creation's sin.

Jesus' heart was cut straight through as He was rejected by His Father, bloodied tears running down His face from His crown of thorns. Mocked as he hung by nail, my Messiah, my Messianic King, gave up His Spirit; the ground shook, and the 'VEIL OF RELIGION' separating me from God was TORN IN HALF FOREVER.

Jesus freely died on a cross for me; Jesus' blood was God's bloodline, poured out to pay the price for my sins to redeem me back to my Heavenly Father. He restored everything. Jesus' broken, beaten, bloodied body was placed alone in a cold, dark empty tomb.

Three days later, He was gone, and the tomb was empty! Jesus rose again by the power of the Holy Spirit, defeating death as the penalty for sin, darkness in hell, and separation from God.

CHAPTER SIXTEEN

UP THE MOUNTAIN

The moment came when I knew I had to decide. I knew it was time; I faced a straightforward question: Did I believe God existed?

> Did I believe God existed?

And at this point, it was like no other question that I had ever encountered before. Unlike other questions with a choice of different answers, this was very different; I now knew the truth, and I could not deny it; there was only one answer in my heart, I now believed.

> The only thing I could think of now was that I had to get right with God!

I went to bed that night, and I dreamed of being knelt on top of a mountain. The following day when I woke up, I recognised this mountain in my dream as it was the one near where I was. I knew I had to go; I believed God was calling me up the mountain. There was a sense of urgency in my Spirit; the only thing I could think of now was that I had to get right with God!

> There was a sense of urgency in my Spirit.

It was the 20th of April, 2017. The mountain near me was around 3,000 meters high and would take me about 4 hours to get to the top.

That morning climb was no ordinary climb; it was like nothing I had experienced before, even on SAS selection; this was not just a physical battle to get to the top; It was everything against me. Voices of doubt, discouragement, and condemnation came against me.

They were condemning me for my past, the mistakes that I had made. Telling me not to go, that I was not going to make it and that I should turn around, the further I climbed, the darker those voices became.

> ...like Jacobs ladder in the harshest of winters

I experienced sickness at one point that I had to press through; what was this trying to prevent me from reaching the top of the mountain? I was not going to turn around; I knew this was a crucial moment in my life.

The final part of the climb was extremely steep; it was like Jacobs ladder in the harshest of winters, entering the cloud; at the top, I fell to my knees and cried out to God.

"I believe! I surrender my life to you, Lord; whatever it takes, whatever it looks like, wherever it is, I will go. "...

> The power of God hit me like nothing I had experienced before in my life!

The devil had taken me into the fire to destroy me and what he did not know was that fire cannot destroy fire. The Shekinah Glory looked like a consuming fire on the mountain. The power of God hit me like nothing I had experienced before in my life.

> Devils were bound by the Word of God and detained on that mountain in Iraq.

As I knelt in tears, broken-hearted and empty, in the glorious presence of Jesus, the fire went through my body as I was delivered, resurrection power tore the strongholds down over my life, and devils were bound by the Word of God, and detained on that mountain in Iraq, my mind was healed, and my Spirit was set free from the darkness and brought into the light as I received 'God's Spirit' in me and was 'Born Again', from 'DEATH to LIFE!'

> I heard Jesus speak deep into my being, 'Evangelist'.

I don't know why God called me to be an evangelist that day on the mountain; He put something deep within me. What I do know is this, the message Jesus has given me to carry within me is one of 'Death to Life,' a coming from out of 'Darkness and into Light' being 'Born Again' and filled with 'God's own Spirit to live your life as a child of God and as a citizen of heaven.

God has taken me on a journey to learn and understand spiritual warfare, of taking down enemy strongholds, into the unreached places, the devils' backyard, in this war against terror, this is my new frontline.

Wherever you are right now, I want you to know that it is not by chance or coincidence that you have read this book; Jesus made a way for you to read it and hear the truth about your eternal life.

This moment is between you and Jesus, and it is a private moment and the most critical moment of your life where you now must decide if you believe.

This decision can not be made by anyone else, only you; there will be no second chances once you have died, and you do not know when you will die; today is the day to make this decision, not tomorrow, but today, not later but now.

The devil is saying tomorrow to delay you, deceive you and steal this moment from you.

Do not let the devil take you to hell, the place of death, permanent torment with weeping and gnashing of teeth, cold darkness eternally separated from the presence of God.

Can you deny what you have read? You must now surely know the truth that it is time for you to step out of the 'DARKNESS' and into the 'LIGHT' and believe, be 'Born Again,' and receive 'God's Spirit.'

If you believe with all of your heart and mind and declare with your mouth that Jesus Christ is your Lord, you shall be saved!

THE CROSS

> The SAS is the world's most elite special forces. I pushed myself physically, mentally, and emotionally to the limits a man could go to. In my pursuit of truth, I pushed myself to my spiritual limit; Jesus, however, went far beyond those limits more than any man has ever gone or could ever go, and He did it for you!

- Kevin Charles-Thompson

KEVIN CHARLES-THOMPSON

ABOUT THE AUTHOR

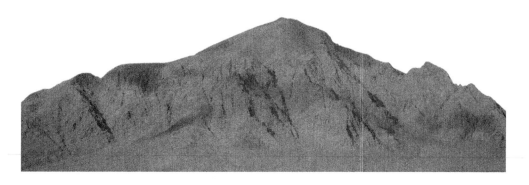

Kevin Charles-Thompson

" I'm from the United Kingdom; I'm 43 years old and married with two children. I served eighteen years in the British Army, finishing my long career in the world's most elite special forces, 22 Special Air Service (SAS).

I have been operationally deployed on counter-terrorism and counter-insurgency operations across the globe, including long campaigns in Northern Ireland, Africa, Iraq, Afghanistan, and Syria, fighting the global war on terror.

During an operational deployment, I seriously injured my knee, requiring surgery. I spent a year in rehabilitation, undergoing extensive physiotherapy, hydrotherapy, and cryotherapy. Rehabilitation was unsuccessful, and after consultations with some of the UK's leading medical experts and knee specialists, I was medically discharged from the SAS as permanently non-deployable.

Kevin, Naomi, Myah and Shekinah

My wife Naomi and I felt led by God to leave the UK and relocate to Cape Town, South Africa, where we spent the next two years as part of a leadership team starting a new church. Within six months of being in Cape

Town, I was back to running, wearing a 20kg weighted training vest; I ran to the top of Lion's Head, a 600-meter mountain, in under an hour; God had completely healed me.

Since returning from South Africa, we moved to the United States to complete the Christ for all Nations (CfaN) School of Evangelism, and I was ordained as a CfaN minister of the gospel. I have recently been on a gospel crusade in Nigeria, Africa.

During the month I was in Nigeria, my team of four preached the gospel to over 10,000 adults and children, and I saw over 7,000 decisions to receive Jesus Christ as their Lord and Saviour. I witnessed God open blind eyes, open deaf ears, and those who were mute spoke for the first time. The crippled started to walk, people were delivered from the demonic and set free, and many more miracles, signs, and wonders occurred.

ABOUT THE AUTHOR

A mountain in Iraq 2017

> I have learned that God is the God of the mountain and the God of the valley; whatever you are facing in your life, no matter what you are going through right now, you can overcome it with Him if you believe. I hope you find the truth, and it sets you free.

SAS EVANGELIST

ABOUT THE BOOK

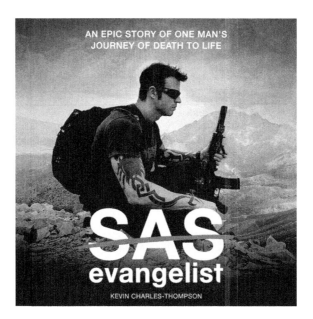

SAS Evangelist

> The Lord called me to write SAS Evangelist to share my testimony.
>
> I have been journeying from being an expert in natural warfare to being schooled in spiritual warfare.
>
> SAS Evangelist is not just an epic story of one man's journey from death to life; it demonstrates the power of the gospel in one man's life. In the unrelenting pursuit of the truth, I was taken on a life-changing journey from the darkness to light.

This book was forged over five years and written through the Holy Spirit to bring the truth to those who have ears to hear.

OUR PARTNERS
DEDICATION

Kevin and Naomi Charles-Thompson

> We want to take this opportunity to honour and thank all of our partners for their willingness and generosity in supporting us on this long journey, from church planting in South Africa to the Christ for all Nations school of evangelism in the United States. A gospel crusade in Nigeria, Fire camps for upcoming evangelists, and publishing this book, which we believe will impact and change many lives around the world, we could not have done it without you.
>
> Thank you, Love, Kevin and Naomi

SCRIPTURE

Scripture quotations are from The ESV® Bible (The Holy Bible, English Standard Version®), copyright © 2001 by Crossway, a publishing ministry of Good News Publishers. Used by permission. All rights reserved.

COPYRIGHT

No part of this book may be reproduced in any form or by any electronic or mechanical means, including information storage and retrieval systems, without written permission from the author, except for the use of brief quotations in a book review.

Copyright © 2022 SAS Evangelist by Kevin Charles-Thompson.

All rights reserved worldwide.

www.sasevangelist.com

Printed in Great Britain
by Amazon

13393792R00102